MW00398667

Evangelical Christians are in urgent need of serious, faithful, and intelligent answers to questions every believer confronts. In this series, Owen Strachan and Gavin Peacock honor the gospel and help believers to understand these urgent questions, to think biblically, and to live faithfully.

Albert Mohler
President, The Southern Baptist Theological Seminary,
Louisville, Kentucky

In this series of books Owen Strachan and Gavin Peacock show us how amazingly relevant the Bible is to our smartphone generation. Technology often only conspires with our wandering and warped passions to leave us in a state of enslavement and despair. However, this trilogy points to God's word as our only hope through its holistic teaching on sexuality and through the gospel of God's redeeming grace. I cannot too highly recommend a prayerful study of these books. They might prove a life-saver!

Conrad Mbewe
Pastor of Kabwata Baptist Church, Lusaka, Zambia

We daily awake to a culture saturated with sexual temptation and confused about sexual identity. Instantaneous and worldwide media accelerate and proliferate these sinful ideologies in an unprecedented way. The Bible, however, provides supernatural power to overcome sexual temptation and divine definition for sexual identity. In this straightforward and powerful series, Strachan and Peacock relay a message of hope, transformation, and biblical recalibration because of Christ. These pages are a reveille bugle to wake up a generation sedated by sinful, sexual trajectories. This series is for pastors, parents, and anyone who desires biblical clarity in a world of confusion.

Rick Holland
Pastor, Mission Road Bible Church, Prairie Village, Kansas

Here is an extremely timely trilogy for the cultural crisis in which we find ourselves. Addressing the issue of human sexuality head on, Owen Strachan and Gavin Peacock have delivered a brilliant analysis of the present day crisis over personal sexuality and gender issues. Not only do they make the right diagnosis, they also prescribe the one and only cure for this devastating problem. They offer the transforming power of the saving and sanctifying grace of God. You need to be conversant with the truths in this trilogy.

Steven J. Lawson
President, OnePassion Ministries
Professor, The Master's Seminary, Sun Valley, California
Teaching Fellow, Ligonier Ministries

I enthusiastically endorse this biblical sexuality trilogy on lust, homosexuality and transgenderism, written by men of conviction, who know what God has revealed in His Word and who understand the sinful struggles of fallen humanity. The authors have courageously written about some of the most sensitive issues of our times, denouncing the deviation from God's original design, while always pointing to the person (Christ) who can give us the victory over such sinful desires and behaviors. If there was ever a generation in need of such a trilogy it is ours. What an insightful and powerful tool this will prove to be for the church of our time. These books are biblical, readable, practical and answer many of the questions many are asking. Every pastor, every leader, in fact, every person who wants to be thoroughly informed about these issues should read this trilogy.

Miguel Núñez
President, Ministerios Integridad y Sabiduría
(Dominican Republic)

Strachan and Peacock confront sexual sin where it begins: in the heart. These men understand that Scripture, by the power of God's Spirit, is the only instrument that can confront the sinful lusts that reside in the dark crevices of the heart. With biblical precision and pastoral care, Strachan and Peacock demonstrate the connection between heart desires and sinful behavior. You would do well to heed their biblical warning and instruction to tackle sinful actions by practically confronting sinful desires with the truth of God.

T. Dale Johnson, Jr.
Executive Director, ACBC
Associate Professor of Biblical Counseling,
Midwestern Baptist Theological Seminary, Kansas City,
Missouri

Our twenty-first century world is deeply confused about the meaning of sex. ... This series directly applies biblical truth to urgent matters of human sexuality, and does so with both pastoral sensitivity and theological integrity. All too often the church fails to respond to sexual sin with both compassion and clarity. This series does both, and does so with courage, verve, and an ever-present reminder that Jesus Christ is making all things new.

David Talcott
Assistant Professor, The King's College, New York

This biblically-centered and theologically-robust series on biblical sexuality is a tour de force. There aren't two other theologians I would rather hear from on these vital issues than Strachan and Peacock. Not only do they bring scholarship to bear on the predominant conversation of our culture, but they offer warm pastoral counsel as they seek to redirect this conversation from the public square back to the foundation of Scripture. If you struggle with sexual sin, deal with questions about sexuality in your current ministry context, or desire to learn more about such issues, this trilogy of books is for you.

Dustin W. Benge
Senior fellow, The Andrew Fuller Center for Baptist Studies
and professor at Munster Bible College, Cork, Ireland

Today people are wandering in a fog of confusion regarding sexuality. Truth cuts through the fog in this series of books from Owen Strachan and Gavin Peacock. They have laid out the simple order of biblical teaching on the most contested debates about sexuality. Testimonies and frequently-asked-questions illustrate the practical usefulness of the bible's teaching. I have witnessed the compassion, wisdom and usefulness of this teaching being applied in Gavin's ministry at our church. The result is that these books are floodlights in the worldly storm. They don't claim to be exhaustive, but neither are they exhausting. They offer much-needed confidence to regular Christians on pilgrimage in this new dark age. But most of all, this trilogy highlights the compassion of Jesus Christ in the gospel. Read these books, share them with others, and let hope pierce the present darkness.

Clint Humfrey
Senior Pastor, Calvary Grace Church, Calgary, Alberta

This is a timely trilogy, and a manly one that ladies will also love. Name three topics hotter than these today in society, and any areas where the Christian home and Church more urgently needs equipping than in matters of gender and sexuality? I've already begun walking through this series with my sons, and it has sparked great discussions. Pastor Peacock and Scholar Strachan form a rare combination and a dynamic duo in this thoroughly biblical response to the 'strong winds of culture' that are blowing. They offer not just a 'battle cry', but also a 'declaration of hope'. With a high view of Scripture and of the local church, and a right view of humanity, they bring gospel remedies and clear answers to the most thorny questions. The FAQs alone are worth the price of each book!

Tim Cantrell
Senior Pastor, Antioch Bible Church & President of Shepherds' Seminary in Johannesburg, South Africa

In a world where sex has become everything, anything, and nothing, Strachan and Peacock do a masterful job at helping the church recover and keep a Biblical theology of sexuality. Their series reminds us that God is the author of life and He has not released His copyright on the creation. Sex is His gift, gender

His distinction, marriage His idea, and true love His nature. Any definition of sexual identity or pursuit of sexual intimacy cannot be rightly achieved apart from obedience to God. As the authors argue, the path to true sexual fulfillment is one decided by the gospel, not our glands. In a sex-crazed world, here are wise words that are timely, truthful, and transformative!

Philip De Courcy
Pastor of Kindred Community Church in Anaheim Hills, California;
Bible teacher on the daily radio program 'Know the Truth'

The terrible times of the last days are dominated by 'feel good' culture which has misled millions onto the destructive super-highway of illicit sex in its different forms. From Scripture, research and the experiences of individuals Peacock and Strachan expose the lies that tried and tested societal norms are bad and 'follow your heart' is good. This series is humble and hard-hitting – saying what needs to be said but which many Christian leaders have been afraid to say. However, this is no mere condemnatory diatribe pointing the finger. These pages are full of compassion. There is practical help for those struggling and a triumphant note that though sexual sin is overwhelming the power of the Lord Jesus Christ is greater. This is a very valuable piece of work.

John Benton
Director for Pastoral Support at the Pastors' Academy, London Seminary, London

Owen Strachan and Gavin Peacock are men full of biblical wisdom and conviction. And that's precisely what the church needs in this hour. The authors bring their wisdom and conviction to bear in this work as they engage some of the most pressing issues confronting the church. I heartily recommend this work to every gospel minister—and the church members they serve.

Jason K. Allen
President, Midwestern Baptist Theological Seminary &
Spurgeon College, Kansas City, Missouri

The gospel of Jesus is good news not only because it secures eternal life for the believer, but also because it transforms this life, here and now. This is no less true with respect to the contested intersection of gender, sex, and identity. In this trilogy, Strachan and Peacock show how the gospel renews fallen sexuality and brings wholeness according to God's good design. Anyone curious about what the Bible teaches on sexuality and what biblical obedience looks like will want to use these pithy volumes to grow and disciple others into faithful maturity.

Colin J. Smothers
Executive Director, Council on Biblical Manhood and
Womanhood

# WHAT DOES THE BIBLE
## TEACH ABOUT
# TRANSGENDERISM?

### OWEN STRACHAN & GAVIN PEACOCK

CHRISTIAN
FOCUS

Copyright © Owen Strachan and Gavin Peacock 2020

hardback ISBN 978-1-5271-0478-5
epub ISBN 978-1-5271-0583-6
mobi ISBN 978-1-5271-0584-3

10 9 8 7 6 5 4 3 2 1

First published in 2020
by
Christian Focus Publications Ltd,
Geanies House, Fearn, Ross-shire,
IV20 1TW, Great Britain

www.christianfocus.com

Cover by Peter Matthess

Printed and bound
by Gutenberg Press Ltd, Malta

# CONTENTS

## Dedication

To Stuart Taylor and Graham Daniels

*Pastors who spoke with two
voices – one to warn the wolves,
one to tend the sheep*

(cf JOHN CALVIN)

*All Scripture is breathed out by God and profitable for teaching, for reproof, for correction, and for training in righteousness, that the man of God may be complete, equipped for every good work.*

(2 Tim. 3:16-17)

# INTRODUCTION

'You are a very fluid concept right now.' As I read the stories about boys entering girls' races, and people suing for the right to enter the washroom of the opposite sex, I sometimes think of this humorous line from a romantic comedy released a few years back. The movie had nothing to do with transgenderism, but as I turn it over in my mind, it seems to sum up life in our time. It arguably captures much of how we are encouraged to think about ourselves in 2020. We're fluid; our identity is malleable; we can be whoever we want to be.

Remember the famous words from another film—the famous movie *Pinocchio*—so long ago, sung in a dreamy way?

> *When you wish upon a star*
> *Makes no difference who you are*
> *Anything your heart desires will come to you*

We can amend this lyric. In one form or another, our culture says to us today: 'Anything your heart desires you can become.' There are no real limits to this promise. No one can tell us who we actually are. We are not created beings who need to know the wise design of our Creator. We are self-creators now, and we should follow our heart above all else.

It's as if the West has updated the famous saying of the philosopher Descartes. You probably remember it from high school: *I think, therefore I am.* In 2020, we say to ourselves: *I feel, therefore I am.* That seems to form the basis of the self today: feelings. This leaves us trying to find stability in the most unstable of places. It's a little like trying to read quietly outdoors as a thunderstorm rages overhead, or having a deep conversation at a football game. Good luck with that! By definition, our feelings change and morph and shift. Looking to our feelings to ground our identity may work for a season, sure, but will not last over the long term. We need something stronger, something surer, something enduring. We need something beyond us.

This is not the only problem with following our feelings. Our feelings-driven mentality sidesteps the whole issue of the morality of our feelings. It's all well and good to say something like: 'I follow my heart, and so I've embraced my authentic self.' We hear this sort of line all around us today. But many questions rise up in response: is our heart *good*? Are our feelings *right*? Should we follow our desires? We need to ponder this one hard. Don't murderers 'follow their heart'? Isn't that what lying politicians and cheating spouses do? Isn't that what we ourselves do when we get angry and verbally lash out at someone, using language that does damage to relationships?

## Don't Follow Your Heart

With questions like these, we can begin to see how problematic it is to trust your feelings. Feelings can be good; feelings can definitely be bad. Following your feelings is unstable at best and personally destructive at worst. But there's more: when we make our feelings our *identity*, we double down on this troubling trend. It's as if we say: Not only should I follow my heart wherever it takes me, but I should make my 'heart'—which is understood as a collection of desires and emotions and inclinations—my personal identity. In other words, let's say I have the feeling that I am a girl trapped in a boy's body. According to our culture's logic, I am right not only to affirm this feeling, to see it as good, but to follow it all the way to its (seemingly) logical conclusion: I must be a girl trapped in a boy's body. This means, to extend the point, that I may well take major and

**17**

possibly irreversible steps to change my body to match my feelings.

This is no fake exercise. This thought process plays out all around us today. For a variety of reasons, and from a plethora of backgrounds, some people experience 'gender dysphoria,' the feeling mentioned above. They wonder if their identity and their body don't match. Responses to this feeling vary today, but our non-Christian culture gives us one strong take: it tells us that if we have such inclinations, we may well be a 'transgender' person, having an identity that is different from our body, and so need to 'transition' to a different body through surgery, medicine, and other means.[1] In such a mentality, we should not rebuke our feelings and thoughts; instead, we should trust them, for they will lead us to the true self-conception that has perhaps long evaded us.[2]

---

1  To better understand the development of the sexual revolution, see R. Albert Mohler, Jr., *We Must Not Be Silent: Speaking Truth to a Culture Redefining Sex, Marriage, and the Very Meaning of Right and Wrong* (Nashville: Thomas Nelson, 2016).

2  See Planned Parenthood's definitions of two terms engaged in this book: '**Gender Dysphoria**: A diagnosis, often used by psychologists and doctors, to describe the distress, unhappiness, and anxiety that transgender people may feel about the mismatch between their bodies and their gender identity. … **Transgender:** A general term used to describe someone whose gender

We also witness softer forms of this thinking. People today show that they buy into the distinction between their feelings and their body when they embrace androgyny. Perhaps they do not go all the way and surgically change their body, but they believe nonetheless that their body is just matter, and they have the freedom to express their true self however they see fit. Societal norms exist to trap people into conformity; better to follow one's feelings over narrow expectations. This quiet belief morphs easily into a full-blown lifestyle and worldview. Here, by contrast, is what we're going to argue in this book: don't follow your heart.[3]

## What We Have Heard About Our Feelings (and Identity) Is Not True

That's just a bit counter-cultural, isn't it? Isn't this a little cheeky – being so contrarian? Some readers might be wondering what we're up to at

---

identity is different than the sex assigned at birth.' Planned Parenthood, 'Transgender Identity Terms and Labels,' accessible at https://www.plannedparenthood. org/learn/sexual-orientation-gender/trans-and-gender-nonconforming-identities/transgender-identity-terms-and-labels. Last accessed January 2020.

3   See Jon Bloom, *Don't Follow Your Heart: God's Ways Are Not Your Ways* (Minneapolis, Minnesota: Desiring God, 2015).

this point, and we can hardly blame then. Are we seeking an argument for its own sake? Goodness knows there's enough of that in our divided times!

Our reason for giving this advice is not because we want to ruin your day. It's not because we're really grumpy about a changing world. It's not because we dislike diversity. We don't want you to follow your heart because we know this biblical truth: the heart is not trustworthy. We're sinners. We should not look to ourselves for cosmic wisdom. Instead, we should go to the very source of wisdom and beauty and hope: God. God has everything we need. So, don't follow your heart, dear reader. Follow God.

Following your heart has many endpoints today. People all around us are seeking wholeness and happiness and acceptance. These are good things to seek. But if we seek them in the wrong places, we will surely reap calamity. This is just what's happening today regarding the LGBTQ movement. People are being told that if they follow their heart, their deepest instincts and desires, they'll be whole and happy and affirmed. But this is not true. We cannot gain wholeness in this fragmented world; we cannot know lasting joy in what the Bible calls sin; we cannot find peace, true peace, outside of God.

Yet the transgender movement—if we can call it that—says we can. It says that we can find what we seek outside of God and His Word. If we will only embrace our truest self, the thinking goes, we'll discover what we've so long sought. This is a key part of why many people, including a good number of women and a high number of men, embrace a cross-gender identity and appearance.[4] They think that they are finding who they truly are. Really, this is a specific version of the life philosophy introduced above and urged everywhere today: follow your heart. Change your body. Gain a new identity.

There is no one-size-fits-all experience along these lines, though. We recognize that many people are profoundly confused today by the political turmoil surrounding the transgender lobby, and we know that there are some people who experience gender dysphoria and don't want it. Further, in some cases, gender dysphoria, cross-dressing, and transgender affiliation is connected to familial breakdown, relational disturbance, unrelieved shame, and pain. We have studied this issue intensively, and we sense that many people who fit the 'transgender' category live in chaos and long for peace.

---

4   Some research indicates that three out of four people who 'transition' are men becoming women. See Femke Olyslager and Lynn Conway, 'On the Calculation of the Prevalence of Transsexualism,' accessible at http://ai. eecs.umich.edu/people/conway/TS/Prevalence/Reports/ Prevalence%20of%20Transsexualism.pdf. Last accessed January 2020.

## Disorienting Orientation: When Christianity Destabilizes a Worldview

This little book thus seeks to lay out the way back to God for people drawn to cross-gender identity and behavior, a major cause (and trap) of our time. Far from being a scold, this book reveals that every person has tremendous dignity and worth and purpose because God made us, and made us for Himself. We will see this in Chapter 1 when we cover Genesis 1-2. This section of Scripture—as with all the Bible—teaches us vital truth about God, humanity, and the world in which we live. The Bible is the very mind and will of God. The Bible is God-breathed, such that every word is inspired by the Holy Spirit; accordingly, the Bible is inerrant, without error in all it teaches; thus the Bible is authoritative, the standard of all standards; so the Bible is fully sufficient, fitted perfectly to purify us and conform us to God's holy standard. The Bible is not one religious book among many, therefore; the Bible is the very Word of God, the truth we need to form a worldview, understand our lives, and live for God's glory.[5]

---

5   To understand this brief theology of Scripture, see texts like Numbers 23:19; Psalm 119; John 1, 8, and 16; 2 Timothy 3:16; 2 Peter 1:3-11, 21. For a readable resource on this doctrine, see J. I. Packer, *Truth & Power: The Place of Scripture in the Christian Life* (Wheaton, Illinois:

In a sinful world, we will resist the biblical witness, however. The fall disordered every person in some sense, and as a result we don't think, feel, or believe as we should. We may have a major struggle with our identity or we may not, but every person loses God in the fall. This plays out differently for every person. Yet the point before us stands: we need God desperately. If we are to escape the pain and broken-ness caused by sin, we must return to the Lord. This is what we will cover extensively in Chapter 2: how the gospel shows us the way back to God. As we will see, this does not mean that we affirm ourselves in our natural state. Whatever trauma may be in our past—and we know that trauma is real and needs compassionate care—we will only find wholeness in the grace of repentance.

Said in a different way, whatever our past, God is gracious to convict us of sin and free us from following our heart. Following our heart may be what our culture encourages us to do, but it is what the Bible calls 'the way of death' (Prov. 14:12; Jer. 21:8).

---

Harold Shaw, 1996). See also the two helpful statements of the International Council on Biblical Inerrancy, one on inerrancy, the other on hermeneutics: http://www.alliancenet.org/the-chicago-statement-on-biblical-inerrancy and http://www.alliancenet.org/the-chicago-statement-on-biblical-hermeneutics. Last accessed January 2020.

## Relearning Life: What the Gospel Accomplishes

In Chapter 3, we will offer practical steps to counter 'gender dysphoria,' transgender instincts, and so on. Note that our guidance is theological and pastoral. In other words, individuals who experience gender confusion in myriad ways need—first and foremost—to know what the Word of God teaches about their body and their identity. The truth of God sorts us all out and puts us back in working order to God's glory. But we do not present this material as if merely studying the Word immediately closes all issues related to gender dysphoria. The gospel is the solution to our sin, but when we believe it and claim Christ as Savior and Lord, God initiates a lifetime of sanctification.

This book approaches the subject of transgenderism directly. We are a partnership, if you will; Owen is a theologian with pastoral concern, and Gavin is a pastor with theological concern.[6] Our

6  Owen has invested much time and energy in researching and writing on these matters, producing scholarship of various kinds on these theological subjects. Gavin has counseled widely in his church, working with people of various sexual sin patterns (and many others besides), and has seen many people affected and changed by God's grace as a result of the application of sound doctrine.

first goal is to give biblical clarity on this subject; our text is not primarily a call to political action or a summons to personal protest, though we believe Christians should speak truth on this issue everywhere they can. It is a work of theology aimed at everyday transformation. Christianity does not center in pleasant feelings and good wishes; it centers first in clarity, in handling the Word of God accurately so that we apply it rightly (2 Tim. 2:15). It is only when we know the truth that we can live rightly before the Lord.

In sum, this is a book about truth even as it is a book about love. But this love is not cheap love; this love is driven by what Dietrich Bonhoeffer rightly called *costly grace*, grace that means you leave the world behind in repentance and faith.[7] What a gift costly grace is; what a gap stands between it and mere affirming love which seeks no change and offers no true hope. Nothing could more bless us than the truth that sets us free so that we might know the love of God. In knowing the love of God, we discover who we are. We know who God made us to be. We gain power over the

---

7   Dietrich Bonhoeffer, *The Cost of Discipleship* (New York: Touchstone, 1995 [1937]), pp. 45-49. We appreciate this insight, even as we note that we cannot endorse Bonhoeffer's theological program comprehensively. When it comes to the nature of history, for example, he must be read with great care.

flesh. We come to understand the meaning of our body.

Humanity is a very fluid concept right now. At least that's the way our fallen culture thinks. But in the mind of God, humanity has meaning and stability. Because of that truth, we all have hope – Godward hope. But to know the depth of that hope, we must know the depth of our sin. To that reality we now turn.

# 1. THE BIBLE ON GENDER AND IDENTITY

Have you ever stopped to think about what a revelation your body is to you?

Perhaps you read that sentence and sigh. You think, *Yes, my body is revealing to me that I need less sweets and more jogging.* Or maybe you say to yourself, *my body is telling me I'm aging – and I don't want to!* We all deal with such matters, it's true. But we don't mean that our body tells us first and foremost a bunch of nagging demands or disheartening details. We mean that the body displays clear evidence of design. There is a designer, an aesthetic Creator who has made us just the way He wants us to look.

As Christians, we believe in what theologians call 'general revelation' and 'special revelation.' We'll talk about special revelation, the witness of Scripture, in a moment.[1] General revelation

---

1   Special revelation can include any direct communication from God to man through media like dreams, spoken

is God's public truth, accessible to all. You don't need faith to see the truths of general revelation; you just need a functioning self. Many of us have heard about how the ocean, mountain cliffs, and starry skies reveal the Lord. How true this is! But fewer of us have thought about how the human body points to divine design. Manhood and womanhood, complementary in nature, tell us a good deal about God's intentions for the human race. The sexes are alike made in God's image, yet the Lord clearly delights in what we could call 'unified diversity.'

The body is a battleground today, the site of so much cultural and political debate. Yet in Scripture, God's revealed Word, the body is not made to cause dissension. The body, as we will see in a moment, is a gift, the gift of God. It is a blessing that tells us much about who we are and who we must be. The body is not a curse, or a sentence of living imprisonment. The body is God's revelation to us of His good will and wise creation order.

---

speech, and more, but in this era of history, we access God's special revelation through the Word of God, the Bible, God's final Word spoken through His Son (Heb. 1). We all need to hear from God, and so it is of special importance that we 'hear' by studying the Bible with all due diligence, not reducing revelation to mystical impressions and special personal words as so many do.

Sadly, many people do not share this understanding of the body. As we covered in the Introduction, they think of the body in very different terms. They think they should fit the body to their true and authentic identity, an identity which may well conflict in major ways with the form and shape of their physical frame. They may go so far as to embrace a 'transgender' identity. People experience what is called 'gender dysphoria'—the feeling of one's body not fitting with one's identity—for many reasons, and those who do need compassionate help to be sure. Their primary need, however, is just what we all most need: the wisdom, plan, correction, and teaching of God.

## Understanding Ourselves in Light of God's Word

In order to help people understand God's design of man and woman, androgyny, and transgenderism, we must go to the Word of God, the one source on planet earth that offers us timeless truth. Strangely, Christians sometimes focus a great deal on what psychologists and doctors say about gender dysphoria and related issues. We do not deny that people who feel like they are trapped in the wrong body need counseling, care, and possibly medical attention. As Christians, we recognize that God made the mind, body, and soul, after all. Yet if we wish to give people hope, we can go nowhere first but the Bible.

The Bible treats our identity in theological and moral terms, as we shall see. God gives us a body in bringing us into this world. His gift of a body tells us who we are: either a boy or a girl, a man or a woman. The Scripture also shows us, however, that people have tried to embrace the identity and appearance of the opposite sex for a very long time. Surely people behave this way for different reasons, and we do well in soul-care and pastoral ministry to tease those out. But we cannot miss that the Scripture expressly forbids what some call 'gender-bending.' There is no holy way to do this; we will only disobey and sin against God by such action.

Christians believe that the Bible is wholly true. It is the very 'God-breathed' revelation God wanted us to have, authored in full by the Holy Spirit (2 Tim. 3:16). The Bible is wholly true, and the Bible is also wholly good in all it teaches (Ps. 19:7). We can go still further, though. The Bible is wholly sufficient. It gives us everything we need for life and godliness (2 Pet. 1:3). We need this affirmation right up front in the conversation over gender dysphoria, transgenderism, and personal identity. While the Word of God never uses the term 'transgender,' it covers the matter with clarity. We will face some hard questions on this subject, yes, but where we need to help people reject cross-dressing and gender-bending, we have. The Word of God is true; the Word of God is good in all it teaches; the Word of God is sufficient for every struggle and spiritual situation we face.

Some may hear these convictions as a battle cry, but they are truly a declaration of hope. This hope is not found in us, in any wise guru, in any activist, in any scientist or doctor, but in God. We have all gone astray in Adam as we shall soon see. Adam's sin is the fountain of 10,000 other sins including our own – the wrong actions we perform, the wicked thoughts we entertain, the sinful impulses we feel in a momentary flash. Praise God that our sin cannot hold us hostage. Through repentance and faith, we gain freedom from the flesh. Through the application of biblical truth, we can overcome our sin.

But we need to know the Word if this victory is to take hold in us. We need to search the Scriptures to understand the divine mind and divine design. When we do so, we will discover that the Bible has a great deal more to say about our trials, temptations, and inner desires than we initially thought. The Bible teaches us much about what some call 'transgenderism,' and it fundamentally tells us to flee it. It makes this point negatively in places as we will note later, and it makes this point positively in the very opening chapters of the Scripture as we now observe.

## Genesis 1-2 and the Glorious Design of Man and Woman

Sometimes the book of Genesis is treated as if it is a creation myth. The early chapters of Genesis, some seem to think, give us a poetic treatment and a spiritualized portrayal of the foundation of the cosmos. While we do glimpse poetic structuring in Genesis 1-2, we come face to face with the actual making of all things. Through His speech and then His action, God makes life. On the sixth day, the apex of all His creative work, God makes man.

Genesis educates us not only about human origins, important as this is, but also about who the human person is created to be. Think of Genesis 1:26-28, which introduces us to humanity, and communicates that humanity is made in God's image:

> Then God said, 'Let us make man in our image, after our likeness. And let them have dominion over the fish of the sea and over the birds of the heavens and over the livestock and over all the earth and over every creeping thing that creeps on the earth.'

So God created man in his own image,
in the image of God he created him;
male and female he created them.

And God blessed them. And God said to them, 'Be
fruitful and multiply and fill the earth and subdue
it, and have dominion over the fish of the sea and
over the birds of the heavens and over every living
thing that moves on the earth' (Gen. 1:26-28).

The first truth of the human person is that our
identity is fixed. We are made by God. At the
creative peak of His work, the Lord chose to
make the man and the woman. He had already
fashioned many aspects of creation, and a good
many creatures, but now He made the one being
that bears His image – His 'own' image, as verse 27
notes. To see the human person, therefore, is to
see a distant reflection of God Himself.

The fact that humanity is made in God's image
means that nothing can alter this reality. The image,
in other words, does not reduce to a certain quality
we possess. The image does not wax and wane in us;
it's not as if some days we more display the likeness
of God, and others we do not. The image does not
rise and fall as our intelligence grows or diminishes.
The image of God is not an ability, so that those who
have more ability in a given area are more human
than others. No, the man is the image and glory of

God, made first by the Lord, and the woman shares full image-bearing status with him (1 Cor. 11:7). Nothing can change this, ruin it, or diminish it. God has said who we are as human beings, and no one can override this identity formation.

Making the man and woman in the image of God means that the Lord has stamped us as spiritual creatures. We have a body, a good and God-formed body, but we are also more than a body. We live an earthly existence, but God created us to transcend our surroundings. We make our home among squirrels and birds and things that creep on the earth, but we have a different identity (and *ontology*, or being, to use a fancy word) than them. They do not bear God's image; we do. All species are not one; God made every creature, so there is a common origin for all things, but the Lord formed humanity alone to know Him in a conscious way.[2] Everything on the earth glorifies the Lord in some way, but only humans bear the capacity to treasure and intentionally reflect the greatness of God.

---

2   He not only made the man conscious of divine presence, but made him covenantally, to know and be known by God. See Thomas R. Schreiner, *Covenant and God's Purpose for the World* (Wheaton, Illinois: Crossway, 2018); Geerhardus Vos, *Biblical Theology: Old and New Testaments* (Carlisle, Pennsylvania: Banner of Truth, 2014 [1948]).

We bear God's image, all of us. This is the first truth about humanity and human identity. The second truth is that God made two sexes from the start: He made the man and the woman. 'Male and female he created them' reads Genesis 1:27, signaling that our manhood or womanhood owes directly to the creative work of the Lord. We cannot source our sex in evolution and evolutionary theory, we see here. Our manhood or womanhood does not trace back to chaos, randomness, luck, chance, or happenstance. There are men and women in the world because God desired that two sexes would bear His image and glorify His name together. By extension, we cannot fail to identify unique value, worth, and dignity in maleness and femaleness. God loves each. God made each. God specially designed each to display, in dazzling form, His wisdom and creativity.

Not only this – God wants His earth filled to the brim with little image-bearers. He called the first man and woman to 'be fruitful and multiply and fill the earth,' Genesis 1:28 says. 'Fruitfulness' here does not mean acting in a colorful way. It has an unmistakably familial bent. *Create a family*, God is saying to the man and woman. *You're not here for yourself. Make lots of little people.* The Lord shows no paranoia about natural resources or overcrowding here; He wants the earth filled, and no two ways about it. *Multiply.* Later we will hear explicitly that children are a 'blessing' and a 'heritage' from the Lord; here the command shows what the Psalms will expand upon (Ps. 127:3). Humanity is not a virus or a plague unleashed upon the earth; the earth was made by God for humanity. It is the main stage for the drama of His glory.

## God's Grand Design: The Callings of Men and Women

Procreation depends upon manhood and womanhood. The man and the woman possess complementary physicality; they alone have the ability to produce children. They each bear the image of God and have full equality as human beings; one is not superior to the other. In Christian theology, we find elegant grounding for unity and oneness as men and women. Yet the Scripture also shows us that men and women have distinct callings, roles, duties, and abilities. Genesis 2 introduces us to these God-honoring distinctions. Let us look briefly at several of them now, for the entire rest of the Bible will build upon this grand design.[3]

---

3   To better understand the grand design of God for humanity, see John Piper and Wayne Grudem, eds., *Recovering Biblical Manhood & Womanhood: A Response*

THE BIBLE ON GENDER AND IDENTITY

*First, the man must protect and work in the garden.* After the Lord makes Adam from the dust of the ground in Genesis 2:7, He gives him his marching orders in Genesis 2:15. The first man must 'work and watch over' the garden, a divine commission that gets our attention in a hurry. We see here the unique importance of work for men; said differently, in biblical terms men are made to work. Men on average have greater strength than women and possess on average 1,000 per cent more testosterone than the fairer sex. These biological realities offer testimony to God's theological blueprint. Men should work. Men will find great joy in working unto God. Work does not proceed from the fall; our working God (for what is *creation* but work?) makes a working man, and the man images the glory of God as he works for his Creator's praise.

The man must also protect the garden. He must 'watch over' it or 'keep' it. Verse 15 tells us both about the man's identity and the garden's status. Though Eden has no corruption nor presence of sin, we do well to pay attention to this detail. The Lord tells Adam here, effectively, that

---

to *Evangelical Feminism* (Wheaton: Crossway, 2006 [1991]); Owen Strachan and Gavin Peacock, *The Grand Design: Male and Female He Made Them* (Fearn: Ross-Shire, Christian Focus, 2016).

he must watch out. Eden is a paradise, made by God Himself, but it is not *perfect*. It is not heaven. The garden needs keeping in the sense that Adam must steward it well, but it also needs keeping because something wicked comes his way. Adam must act as a protector of Eden and of his wife. He must pay attention; he must keep his eyes open; he must not fail to fight off threats that slither across his path.[4]

*Second, the woman has the identity of helper.* There is something 'not good' about Eden, it turns out. The man lives alone (v. 18). This isn't the way God wants it, as we have already seen. He wants a garden—and beyond it a planet—that teems and pulses with life, human life. To accomplish this end, He makes 'a helper' for the man (vv. 18, 20). The woman has a distinct role. God looks at His first human creation, the man, and effectively says, 'He needs help.' He *must* need help, for he cannot 'multiply' by himself. He can only obey the creation mandate of Genesis 1:26-28 with a partner – but more than a partner, a *wife*. It is 'not good' for him to dwell by himself when the Lord made him for marriage, for procreation, for the family.

---

4  See Raymond Ortlund, Jr., 'Male-Female Equality and Male Headship,' in *Recovering Biblical Manhood & Womanhood*, p. 100.

So the Lord makes a woman. She dazzled Adam from the first. Brought to him, the woman's beauty caused the man to cry out 'This at last is bone of my bone, and flesh of my flesh!' (Gen. 2:23). He recognizes instantly that she fits him, complements him, and gladdens him. She will indeed help him; they will produce children together, and she will make a life with him. Under his leadership—signaled by his naming of her as Eve (v. 23)—she will assist him in the filling and subduing of the earth. She alone can bear and nurture life; just as Adam's body tells him his duties, she has a body fitted to her role and duties. She has the vocation of bringing life into the world, human life, and caring for that life so it flourishes and honors the Lord. She alone can give birth; she alone can nurture life physically. We learn much about a woman's calling in general terms from the general revelation of her body (as with the man). She will exhibit numerous strengths and abilities as texts like Proverbs 31 reveal, but her vocation as wife and mother factor in hugely at this point in the biblical narrative.[5]

---

5   For excellent resources on the distinctive beauty and calling of godly womanhood, see Edith Schaeffer, *The Hidden Art of Homemaking* (Carol Stream, Illinois: Tyndale House, 1985); Elisabeth Elliot, *Let Me Be a Woman* (Carol Stream, Illinois: Tyndale House, 1999 [1976]).

*Third, the man bears responsibility for the marriage relationship.* The man is called of God to leave father and mother and 'hold fast' to his wife (v. 24). We cannot take these words as anything but formative for all times and places. Divine design matters, in other words, not only for Adam and Eve, but for all peoples. As we have seen, manhood and womanhood entail not only a certain form and biology, but the assumption of specific roles and the performance of certain tasks by men and women. In Genesis 2, the man has the responsibility to break away from his family, thus embracing maturity in the form of familial leadership, and the responsibility once he has left home to keep his new family together. He must not leave his wife; he must not drift apart from her; he must not release his loving grip on his children. In all respects, he must *hold fast*, showing himself by God's power to be a pillar, a rock, a demonstration of godly strength.[6]

As we discussed in Book Two of this trilogy, God gave the gift of sex to the man and woman – to a husband and a wife specifically. Nakedness comes

---

6   This calling applies to men called to marriage. But as with all teaching on divine design, such material also shapes the character of every man in some form (or every woman, conversely). By extension from this verse, men should be tough, enduring, and loyal. This is the wisdom and plan of God for humanity for all time.

after the garden marriage ceremony of Genesis 2:23; sex is a celebration of God's goodness to the first couple. No shame flows when a man marries a woman and the two enjoy God's blessing of intimacy. The man has a body fitted to the woman, and the woman has a body fitted to the man. There is no need for bodily change or alteration in this scene; God has designed husband and wife to come together, know physical delight, and experience union that goes beyond momentary bliss. All this is good; all this meshes with God's good plan; all this gives glory to God, as one man and one woman taste the delight intended for them by their kind Maker.

## What Goes Wrong: Genesis 3 and the Corruption of Design

We learn much about men and women in Genesis 1-2. But our education does not stop there. In the real historical fall of Genesis 3, and the fallout that follows, we learn why we all naturally stray from God's good plan for the sexes. The serpent shows up on the scene, tempts Eve to believe his promises over God's, and questions God's goodness. Meanwhile, to his everlasting shame, Adam stands passively by (see vv. 1-5). The two eat the forbidden fruit, the fruit from the tree of the knowledge of good and evil, and in so doing bring judgment upon themselves and their offspring (v. 6). Though creatures, the man and woman seek the seat that is God's alone to hold. They forget the infinite gap between themselves and the Lord, and plunge into sin and shame and ruin as a result.[7]

There are many dimensions to the fall, and we have covered some of them in our other books in this trilogy. For the purposes of this text, we will note just a few matters here. First, the fall is a physical fall that triggers physical consequences. The woman takes a physical substance, and thus allows the flesh to have mastery over her soul. The man fails to protect his wife; he should have rebuked the serpent and enacted violence against the snake, but he only stands to the side, passively eating forbidden fruit as his wife directs him (v. 6). He has not kept the command of the Lord; he has not 'watched over' Eden (see Gen. 2:15). With Eve, he has allowed the creation to rule the Creator.

The fall does indeed 'enlighten' the man and the woman in a wicked way. Verse 7 tells us this plainly: 'Then the eyes of both were opened,

---

7   This is called the Creator-creature distinction. Most associated with theologian Cornelius Van Til, it's a very important theological concept introduced in Genesis 1-2 that runs throughout the whole of the Bible. See Van Til, *The Intellectual Challenge of the Gospel* (Phillipsburg, NJ: Presbyterian and Reformed Publishing Co., 1980), p. 19.

and they knew that they were naked. And they sewed fig leaves together and made themselves loincloths.' Few verses in the Bible matter more for our consideration, our study in this little book, than this one. Eating the fruit brings awareness of nakedness and—for the first time—shame over this nakedness. The man and the woman previously did not regard their bodies as a problem, but now they do. Now they must cover themselves. They seem to feel exposed spiritually, and they reflect this insecurity in their physical action. They take a second physical action to their sin and hide themselves (or try to) from the Lord (Gen. 3:8). Surely much is transpiring here, but we cannot miss the obvious truth in this terrible play-by-play: spiritual rebellion produces physical covering and hiding. Simply put, spiritual sin has physical effects.

The body made by God for His glory now seems repugnant. In addition, the earth made to put God's greatness on display now seems best for hiding. The body has been used wrongly to transgress God's command; the creation is now used wrongly to conceal disobedient humanity. We do not mean at this juncture that Adam and Eve experience what we would call 'gender dysphoria,' feeling as though they have a different 'gender identity' than their body. We do, however, take pains to note that sin against God—the act of eating fruit, a physical act plotted by the heart—leads to two distinct physical actions, both of which involve misuse of God's creation.

In response to this act of pride and rebellion, the Lord shows up. He pronounces a judicial sentence on the serpent, the woman, and the man in that order. All three will bear physical effects of the curse. The serpent will slide on its belly in the dust before its head is crushed by the woman's seed (v. 15 – a foretelling of the coming of Christ). The woman will vie for her husband's role and face terrible pain in childbearing (v. 16). The man will navigate great hardship in working the ground, encountering discomfort, difficulty, and eventually dust as he dies (vv. 17-18). The creation is cursed now. The good design of God stands, and no one can undo it. But those made to know the Lord and serve His purposes will now use their bodies and their very lives to dishonor God.

They will do this by rejecting God's wiring of their bodies, their male and female identities, and their relationships. Made according to God's wisdom, they will turn away from it and fashion their own self-conception. Though fashioned in the image of God, they will deny any connection to the Creator, and even use their God-given intelligence to deny His making. Though formed a man or woman for His glory, they will reject the idea that sex has a certain meaning and purpose. Given a distinct identity by God, they will reject God-designed 'nature' and creation order (Rom. 1:26), and instead argue that every person is a blank slate, and we all must create our own identity.[8] Made as the beautiful union of a soul and body (an embodied soul, truly), they will try to separate the soul and the body, severing any connection between the two, leaving the body only raw, moldable matter in the end. Called by God to certain duties and roles according to their sex, they will decry created order and seek to make their own neo-pagan order.

Tragically, these effects play out before us today. In some cases this is true without us knowing it or even being aware of these problems. Children grow up with little sense of the meaning of manhood and womanhood. They wear 'gender-neutral' clothes that dampen down

---

8   French theologian Henri Blocher notes the connection between depravity and denial of creation order: 'Evil is not in the good that God has created, but in the rejection of the order that God has instituted for the enjoyment of the world.' Henri Blocher, *In the Beginning: The Opening Chapters of Genesis* (Downers Grove: InterVarsity, 1979), p. 140. If we do not have a strong doctrine of divine design, God-created nature, and creation order, the strong winds of culture will surely threaten to unmoor us and capsize our Christian worldview.

their boyhood or girlhood. We call fathers and mothers the generic term 'parents' (perhaps without a second thought or ill intention) and see fathers and mothers as essentially the same. Young men wear the clothes and adopt the hairstyle of young women; young women wear the clothes and adopt the hairstyle of young men. Gender androgyny now represents the vanguard of modern culture, while holding to any hard-and-fast understanding of maleness and femaleness seems increasingly ancient and discredited.

It can feel quite disheartening to love God's design today. This holds true not only in the godless culture, but in the church. We talk much today about what biblical complementarity is *not*, and may feel great concern when asked to state what it *is*. In too many churches, the people hear little preaching and teaching in detail about the sexes. Small wonder, then, that Christians today have little sense of how to respond not only to transgenderism, but to gender androgyny more broadly. Too few saints have heard a joy-fueled vision of life as a man or woman of God. We will talk in much greater detail about this vision in Chapters 2 and 3. For now, it is enough to note that many feel uninformed when it comes to these important matters.

We have tried to help thus far. We have lined out some of the basic truths about pre-fall humanity and post-fall humanity with respect to the body and personal identity. In what follows, we will observe several key teachings and moments in the rest of Scripture that show us that the biblical authors speak with one voice about the goodness of embracing our God-given body. To put it the opposite way, the Scripture also shows us just how significant rejecting our body, and bodily personhood, truly is. Doing so in the end is nothing less than sinful rebellion against the Lord, rebellion of an all-too-familiar kind.

## Your Cloak Matters: Deuteronomy 22 on Cross-Dressing

Thus far we have largely sketched foundations for the topic of this book. Surprisingly, the Bible dives into the issue of gender-bending very early on, all the way back in the time of the Pentateuch (the first five books of the Bible). Deuteronomy 22:5 says this: 'A woman shall not wear a man's garment, nor shall a man put on a woman's cloak, for whoever does these things is an abomination to the LORD your God.' Right smack in the middle of a list of abominable (very ungodly) behavior, the old covenant law speaks clearly. God prohibited in the clearest possible terms the presentation of an opposite-sex identity. Thousands of years ago, well before modern gender advocacy, the Bible shuts down the possibility of gender-bending.[9]

This text likely responds to numerous issues faced by ancient Israel several thousand years ago. The law of the Old Testament declared God's moral will and helped the covenant people of the Lord distinguish what honored their Maker from what did not. We should not, after all, think that only the Israelites existed in the ancient world; far from it. Many people lived around Israel, and they did not worship Israel's God, and thus they did not follow God's design. We have evidence of pagan sexual practices in Babylon, for example, in which men and women would swap identities in their romantic encounters. Swapping and 'mixing' happened frequently in the ancient near east, as

---

9    Midwestern Seminary scholar Jason DeRouchie com-
     ments on the Hebrew in this passage: 'God chose to
     frame these prohibitions as durative, so that we should
     read the "not" as a "never": "A woman shall never wear
     a man's garment, nor shall a man ever put on a woman's
     cloak".' Jason S. DeRouchie, *How to Understand and
     Apply the Old Testament: Twelve Steps from Exegesis to
     Theology* (Phillipsburg, New Jersey: P&R, 2017), p. 445.
     DeRouchie's section on this passage should be read and
     pondered by every pastor; it is the best short scholarly
     treatment of transgender in print.

godless tribes used the earth however they saw fit, not how God intended it to function.

Old Testament scholar Eugene Merrill points out that using things wrongly is the theme of this section of Deuteronomy: dress (v. 5), animals (vv. 6-7), house (v. 8), field (v. 9), animals (v. 10), dress (vv. 11-12).[10] Using the God-made world wrongly angered God in the strongest possible terms. So far from the idea of God as caring only about our heart, this section of Deuteronomy shows us, beyond a shadow of a doubt, that the Lord cares profoundly about how humanity engages creation. Some of the prohibitions and directions sound strange to modern ears, but if studied with care and sensitivity, we learn that Yahweh received worship in the smallest possible ways – not mixing fabrics in one's dress, for example, as the lost tribes did.

Our God is a God of the big and of the small. He desired His people to set themselves apart in a decisive and comprehensive way. The Israelites could not live however they wanted; they had a certain calling, a way of life, that the Lord laid out in His law. This law no longer binds the new covenant people of God, but it does show us in

10  Eugene H. Merrill, *Deuteronomy*, vol. 4, The New American Commentary (Nashville: Broadman & Holman Publishers, 1994), pp. 297-298.

powerful terms that God cares about even the seemingly minor matters of our everyday lives.

The law distinguished clearly between the Israelites and the pagans. The pagans believed in many gods, not one; they blurred sexual boundaries, and did not respect God's plan for marriage; they sacrificed their children to appease the gods, and did not protect their children from evil; they worshipped the creation, not the Creator; they saw no problem with switching their self-presentation to that of the opposite sex, not following God's clear construction of what is *natural* and what is *un-natural* (see Rom. 1:18-32). The pagans rejected a belief in created order of most any kind, not seeing order as a good gift of the Lord.

Cross-dressing then and now is no neutral practice. Cross-dressing fits seamlessly into pagan spirituality. It is deeply and irreversibly wrong. It offends God on a personal level. It draws the term 'abomination' in Deuteronomy 22. It is a sin that offends not only God's will, but God's design. Cross-dressing exists because belief in God-designed 'nature' does not. If you do not believe that God created manhood and womanhood, then you need not present yourself as a man or woman. You have complete freedom to embrace whatever identity you most prefer, and to change that self-conception as you see fit. After all, there is no Creator, there is no clear law to guide your life, and there is no blessing for obedience and cursing for sin.

But cross-dressing cannot fit into Christianity. Christianity teaches that God made humanity according to His own wisdom and plan. He made men and women to image His glory in distinct and complementary ways. A man honors God when he looks like a man, Deuteronomy 22 teaches us. Accordingly, a woman honors God when she looks like a woman. The Bible gives us no in-between option, no boundary-crossing category. The appearance we put forth mirrors the truth the Scripture teaches us from its first page: that God made *only* men and women. No other 'gender identity' exists.[11]

In ancient Israel as in the modern West, we all exist as either a man or a woman. Sin does blur these realities, yes, and our biology does get warped in places following the fall. But there is no third gender option allowable by the Word of God. Further, we have no ability to change

---

11  The words of DeRouchie ring out here: 'In Deuteronomy 22:5, loving others and God means that people will maintain a gender identity that aligns with their biological sex and will express this gender in a way that never leads to gender confusion in the eyes of others.' DeRouchie, *How to Understand and Apply the Old Testament*, p. 448.

our gender. Today we must live in the terms laid down so long ago, and not sin against God by denying divine design in a personal and bodily way. 'Transgenderism' is a new term for an old sin. If we wish to honor Scripture, we cannot fail to see that the Word of God spoke to this issue long, long ago. Much as many either ignore or deny this truth, the Word still speaks.

## Jesus Believed in the Binary: Matthew 19 and the Sexes

In our rapid-fire survey, we move from the Old Testament to the New. At some points in the conversation over gender, we hear that Jesus never engaged 'transgender' as an issue. For this reason, the church can hold whatever position it sees fit; it can affirm 'transgender Christianity,' because Jesus never spoke against it. In truth, however, Jesus did speak to the goodness and enduring nature of God's design for humanity. In Matthew 19, He encountered the questions of the Pharisees about divorce. They sought to trap and test Him. Jesus wriggled out of the trap and took the opportunity to honor the Creator's plan for marriage and the family:

> And Pharisees came up to Him and tested Him by asking, 'Is it lawful to divorce one's wife for any cause?' He answered, 'Have you not read that he

who created them from the beginning made them male and female, and said, "Therefore a man shall leave his father and his mother and hold fast to his wife, and the two shall become one flesh"? So they are no longer two but one flesh. What therefore God has joined together, let not man separate' (Matt. 19:3-6).

The Son of God here tells us that the material of Genesis 1-2 is historical fact. The early chapters of the Bible, chapters we covered in some detail, map out God's intention for the sexes. God never desired that marital unions would crumble. He made marriage as a lifelong covenant. Christ affirms the ancient blueprint for the creation of a marriage and a new family: a man leaves father and mother, holds fast to his wife, and the two become one. Jesus underlines this last truth: husband and wife must not think of themselves as two independent sexual contractors who have signed a deal with one another to exchange relational goods and services for a provisional period. Our culture teaches us this sort of view of marriage in different ways. Marriage as many understand it today functions as a temporary partnership of two people whose interests coincide in the present. What will happen in the future? No one can say for sure.

Jesus holds the view that manhood and woman-hood represent core realities of this world. God made the human race this way from the beginning. Marriage depends upon, and is made for, the sexes. Marriage cannot take on any form we wish it to; you cannot edit and tweak it. You can no more change marriage than you can change manhood and womanhood. The reason for this: God made all these things. He made the man; He made the woman; He united them in a lifelong, one-flesh covenant. No one should separate this loving union. *What therefore God has joined together, let not man separate*, Jesus said in His summary comment on God's design for marriage.

This portrait of marriage teaches us much about identity and sexuality. We need to know that what God sets up, what God establishes and institutes, gives us His final word on the matter. In other words, though skeptics sometimes allege that the Bible says nothing about polygamy (and so the Bible leaves open the option for wicked behavior), the Word of God actually speaks with piercing clarity on the matter of holy sexuality (as Book Two covered). God's plan for sex in both the Old and New Testament centers squarely in one-man, one-woman marriage. Jesus' words in Matthew 19 show this in spades. So too with the issue of 'gender identity.' We must not think that Jesus has no word to say about this matter. He tells us quite succinctly that God has made men, and God has made women. We have no other options on the matter.

We cannot therefore endorse any form of androgynous Christianity, nor any form of 'transgender Christianity.' The Father and the Son alike love humanity. They put their word behind the sexes. The teaching of Genesis 1-2 and Matthew 19 (which affirms the former) shows us that Scripture honors and nowhere downplays the sexual 'binary.' The sexes are made to face one another; God makes us all with what we call *complementary reciprocity.*[12] God made men and women to live together. Marriage represents the endpoint of

---

12  We introduced this concept as part of a five-fold outline of biblical sexuality in Book One of this trilogy. Here is that scheme in simplified form. First we can identify *complementary unity.* Here we mean what we introduced above: that the man and the woman are made in God's image (Gen. 1:26-28). Secondly, we can identify *complementary polarity* in biblical sexuality. Here we mean that the sexes—though fully unified—are made distinct by God. Thirdly, *complementary reciprocity* means that the sexes face one another and thus Christian men and women, whether married or single, prize the gifting each sex bears for different life callings and tasks. Fourthly, we must also speak of *complementary interest.* By this we mean that as many boys and girls come of age, they may find an interest in the opposite sex developing in them (see Song 8:4). Lastly, we believe the Bible commends a *complementary desire for marriage.* The desire to be married, including the hope of one-flesh union in a righteous way, is good.

this plan, but even if called to singleness, we still must engage women as women, and men as men. We do not treat either Christians or non-Christians as if they have no sex. They do. This matters, as we shall see in pages ahead.

## Hair and Holiness: Paul's Teaching About the Sexes in 1 Corinthians 11

The New Testament gives us great wisdom through the clarifying teaching of Christ about marriage and divorce. But there is more on this count that we may harvest in our quest for biblical wisdom. In 1 Corinthians 11, the Apostle Paul teaches the church about God's desire for men and women. His words ran counter to the culture of ancient Corinth, a pagan city. They surely run counter to our culture today as well:

> But I want you to understand that the head of every man is Christ, the head of a wife is her husband, and the head of Christ is God. . . . For a man ought not to cover his head, since he is the image and glory of God, but woman is the glory of man. For man was not made from woman, but woman from man. Neither was man created for woman, but woman for man. That is why a wife ought to have a symbol of authority on her head, because of the angels. Nevertheless, in the Lord woman is not independent of man nor man of

woman; for as woman was made from man, so man is now born of woman. And all things are from God. Judge for yourselves: is it proper for a wife to pray to God with her head uncovered? Does not nature itself teach you that if a man wears long hair it is a disgrace for him, but if a woman has long hair, it is her glory? For her hair is given to her for a covering (1 Cor. 11:3, 7-15).

Paul covers a great deal of ground in these verses. We will zero in on a few salient matters. First, he unfolds here the order of creation, a subject he treats as well in 1 Timothy 2:9-15. Here, he connects headship to the Trinity, showing us that the Father is the head of Christ, Christ is the head of every man, and the husband is the head of his wife. In contra-distinction to pagan religion and a pagan worldview, our world exists as an ordered world. God has made all things well, and all things make sense in Him.

Paul focuses most in this passage on the husband-wife relationship. He teaches the doctrine of male headship which has special reference to the context of marital union. Paul desires per his Spirit-given knowledge of divine things that men and women present themselves differently. The man fills the role of 'head' or authority (synonymous with leadership), while the woman displays a unique beauty as woman. The sexes distinguish themselves from one another according to Paul by the length of their hair; it is a 'disgrace' for a man to have 'long hair,' while it is the woman's 'glory' to do the same (vv. 14-15). Bodily presentation of this kind images the order of creation, showing that the husband was created first and has the role of head. This was essential teaching in ancient Corinth, which was a hotbed of anti-design acting and dressing.[13]

We fallible readers must approach this infallible passage with care, this we know. Some of Paul's words seem harder to unpack than others (the reference to the angels, for example). Commentators differ over some of the precise meanings of these verses. Nonetheless, we can glean with certainty here that the Apostle Paul directs us to honor the Lord by our personal presentation of our sex. A man has the body of a man, and should represent himself accordingly by having a different hair length than a woman. A woman has the body of a woman, and should represent herself accordingly by having a different hair length than a man (as

---

13 Corinth 'was a major centre of the Dionysian cult, a religion where male adherents would don feminine apparel in imitation of the god himself, who was closely associated with feminine clothing – the other name by which he is known, Bacchus, is derived from the word bassara, a woman's dress (Farnell 1971, p. 160).' Gillian Townsley, 'Gender Trouble in Corinth: Que(e)rying Constructs of Gender in 1 Corinthians 11:2-16,' *The Bible and Critical Theory* 2 (2), p. 177.

much as she can given her age, that is). In Paul's mind, these matters unveil God's own wisdom. Every time godly men and women own and honor their birth sex in their own distinct culture, they honor the Lord who made them either a man or a woman for His glory.

This teaching flies in the face of our modern gender-neutral culture. As we have noted, many men grow their hair long, and many women cut their hair short. They do so because they see no greater meaning in their sex. Beyond this, men wear the clothing of women, while women do the reverse. Furthermore, the sexes embrace the character traits of the opposite sex, speaking and acting against the teaching of nature and the Word of God. Small wonder that many around us reject 'gender roles.' In truth, our rebellion against 'gender roles' begins long before we ever start discussing who will stay home with the children, who will do the housework, who has responsibility to protect the family, and who is the leader of the home. If we dislike the details of complementarity—of owning our God-given identity as a man or a woman—we will surely dislike the bigger picture.

## The State of Nature: Things We Must State

We need to reframe our thinking about the sexes. The details of manhood and womanhood factor in heavily to a life that either rejects God's design or celebrates God's wisdom. We are not naturally Christians. We naturally hate God and reject Him (see Rom. 3). Not everyone rebels against the Lord in exactly the same way, but the Apostle Paul teaches us that many fall prey to the dishonoring of God's 'natural' design. As made clear in Romans 1:18-32, we not only fail to worship God, we go on to worship the creation. We make our own logic, our own rules, and our own religion. Because we push away from the Creator due to our sinful heart, we also push away from the natural order that God has made. Paul tells us precisely this in Romans 1:26, teaching that the Gentiles despise what he calls 'nature.' They exchange 'natural relations' of the complementary kind for 'unnatural' sexual relations. This awful exchange roots in the overthrowing of God's design of the sexes. Men adopt the sexual role of a woman in a homosexual encounter or relationship, and women do the same (see Rom. 1:26-27).

We can draw a direct line between the full-scale display of depravity in Romans 1 and the details of 1 Corinthians 11. Unnatural sexuality starts with unnatural identity. When you think of yourself as having a different identity than your body, you sever your sexuality from the 'natural' order. Your thinking about yourself is unnatural,

THE BIBLE ON GENDER AND IDENTITY

and so your sexual practice is calibrated to the strong possibility of unnatural sexual practice. This is not to say that these matters always hang together; they do not. But neither can we fail to notice how Romans 1 connects these matters, and how 1 Corinthians 11 teaches us to stay sharp in ways great and small.[14]

Before our bodily rebellion against God reaches the depths of homosexual encounter or embracing a 'transgender' identity, we confront many choices each day on this count. Here are some issues we must all sort through and handle well:

1) Do we love God's design?

2) Do we hunger to display the unique glory of God in our body as a man or a woman?

3) When there are gray areas, do we try to err on the side of embracing our sex?

---

14  Two scholars explain the import of Paul's words in 1 Corinthians 11: 'Whatever is appropriate for the man would be inappropriate for the woman—and vice versa. This strict antithetical relationship seems to suggest that "[c]lear gender boundaries is the point".' Roy E. Ciampa and Brian S. Rosner, *The First Letter to the Corinthians*, The Pillar New Testament Commentary (Grand Rapids, MI; Cambridge, U.K.: William B. Eerdmans Publishing Company, 2010), p. 513.

4) Do we profess to love God's design, but then make decisions over details that express the opposite?

5) When we look at our lives, are we straying into unhealthy patterns such that we could possibly drift into full-blown rejection of our God-given sex?

Every one of us must ponder these kind of questions. The Scripture teaches us in both the Old and New Testaments that our faithfulness to God's creation of our body is a matter of obedience and worship. In Deuteronomy 22, men and women were forbidden in the strongest possible terms— abomination language!—from cross-dressing. In 1 Corinthians 11, men and women were called by an apostle to present themselves according to their God-given sex. The body matters greatly in both the Old and New Testaments, we see. We do not have freedom as non-Christians think they do to dress, present, and act however we see fit. We have a calling from on high to give God glory as a man or a woman – to love being a man or a woman.

This calling extends throughout our person and our life. We must not read the material investigated in this chapter as only speaking to action or behavior. Instead, we should recognize that what the Scripture prohibits in action it also prohibits in identity, thought, desire, and feeling. If it is wrong to do it, it is wrong to desire it. Applying this to issues of the body, we cannot fail to see that Scripture speaks in the strongest terms against adopting cross-gender identity, appearance, and behavior. Even if we never take steps to 'transition' to the opposite sex, our quiet thoughts and private desires for ungodly ends require confession and repentance each and every time we experience them. Our desires are not wrong because they are especially potent or long-lasting; they are wrong because they are focused on ungodly ends, not God's will (see 1 Cor. 10:6).

The comprehensive biblical picture sketched here thus summons us to reject cross-gender thinking, desiring, feeling, and acting. We must *go against* what comes naturally to us if we innately have these passions and instincts.[15] We cannot turn

---

15 Over 1,500 years ago, Augustine understood that we fight an internal battle with ourselves: 'It is called the law of sin because it urges and—so to speak—orders us to sin, and if one obeys it with the mind, one sins without excuse. It is called sin because it was produced by sin and it longs to commit sin. Its guilt is removed by rebirth; the conflict with it is left for our testing. It is an evil; that is obvious.' Augustine, 'Unfinished Work in Answer to Julian,' in *Answer to the Pelagians, III*, vol. 25 of Part I – *Books, The Works of Saint Augustine: A Translation for the 21st Century*, ed. John E. Rotelle, trans. Roland J. Teske (Hyde Park, NY: New City Press, 1999), p. 13; cited

away from the biblical word on gender-bending. It is not right in action, nor is it right in mind, heart, and soul. Scripture calls us to a very high standard, and to see that a life of holiness means the forsaking of every unrighteous instinct. What did Paul say? 'Put to death, therefore, what is earthly in you' (Col. 3:5). To reject 'transgender' identity, feeling, and behavior is very much a death. But it is not only this: it is the beginning of life, spiritual life itself, for all who turn away from it as from every sin, every temptation, every wicked way we conceive of our identity.

You could say it this way: whatever our battle with the flesh, when we die to sin, we live to Christ.

## Concluding Thoughts

The Bible clearly closes off the possibility of adopting a 'transgender' identity. We were made either a man or a woman by God. Our body does not lie to us. It tells us who we are, and it tells us who God wants us to be. The Scripture nowhere endorses the blurring of the lines of our body. In both the Old and New Testaments, men and women receive a divine summons to steer clear of androgynous, gender-bending decisions and actions. The Bible

in Jared Moore, 'A Biblical and Historical Appraisal of Same-Sex Attraction,' PhD Thesis, The Southern Baptist Theological Seminary, 2019, p. 44.

makes the point quite plain: men glorify God by presenting themselves as men. Women glorify God by presenting themselves as women.

Unlike the people who surrounded the church in Corinth, and unlike the people who surround us today, we have no option to break with our body and remake our identity. We honor the Lord and live a holy life when we, in our own distinct culture, embrace our God-given manhood and womanhood. The truth, however, is that every sinner of every kind in some way pushes against God's design. We are all like Adam and Eve in that we do not naturally love God's plan. It grates on us. We do not want the wisdom of the divine. We do not celebrate divine order, and we do not rejoice in creational design.

Praise God, though we stray from the Lord just as Adam did, God has not left us to ourselves. We dwell in ruin and chaos of our own making, but the Lord has intervened. We will see this in Chapter 2; as we go there, we do well to remember not only how Adam and Eve physically rebelled against the Lord and experienced shame over their bodies as a result, but how God stepped in to show them mercy. Even as Eve gave birth, bringing life into the world despite the fall, so the Lord made clothing for the man and the woman from animal skins, from the sacrifice of a life (Gen. 3:21). The solution, ultimately, to their rebellion and their bodily shame was this dying and this clothing. So, too, is the solution for we who rebel—and rebel in our bodies against God—the death of the Son and the clothing of the repentant in His righteousness.

To that gospel truth we now turn.

# 2. RETURNING TO BIBLICAL MANHOOD AND WOMANHOOD

Each year on Christmas Day Leslie comes to spend the day with the Peacock family. He's seventy years old, single and a member of our church. He has led a very interesting life. He was part of a rock band in Manitoba when he was younger, and worked as a sales representative for the *Calgary Herald*. Leslie also entered a transgender lifestyle in the 1990s from which the Lord dramatically saved him.

I know Leslie quite well and asked him if he would share his story with our readers. We'll take a slight detour as we begin this chapter to hear this powerful testimony, which relates so closely to the material we'll cover later in the chapter:

My struggle with my besetting sin began when I was very young. As a boy of around nine or ten I began to dress in my mother's clothes. This was a very unique experience that I found I really enjoyed. I actually remember praying that God would do a miracle and turn me into a girl. When I was about twelve, an older male teenager sexually abused me one time. It wasn't something that I really wanted to repeat. Over the years I realized this and the cross-dressing was not something that God would be pleased about. Through most of my life whenever something would come on TV regarding transvestitism, knowing my weakness in this area I would change the channels.

Throughout my growing up, I continually would practice self-stimulation, which I had discovered on my own, when I was eleven or twelve. I also entered into the use of pornography at this time. My dad owned a drug store and I would steal magazines off the rack. I liked girls and through my teen years I desired to have a girlfriend like all my buddies. Being a young man of over 200lbs I didn't believe any girl would go out with me. I began to loathe and hate myself because I was fat. As a result I developed a very low self-esteem.

My wicked desires were hidden from everyone around me. After all I was a Christian who would fall once in a while, and in my conviction promptly repent and ask God for forgiveness. I would destroy my pornography and carry on with my God. During the late 1960s and early 1970s I moved to Calgary, Alberta and became involved in the Jesus People movement and went to a local in-church Bible College. I really didn't have any hope that anybody would ever want to marry me. That all changed when my Pastor told me that a certain girl in the church wanted to marry me. I had no previous interest in her, but under the circumstances, my interest peaked. After all, I wanted to be married and here was a woman that I knew ahead of time would say yes if I popped the question. And she did. On July 7th of 1977 I got married for the wrong reasons.

We were married for twenty years and adopted two children, a boy and a girl. Throughout the whole twenty years we were faithful in church—two services every Sunday—and also taught Sunday school classes. I guess I was looked up to as a well-respected member of our church, but underneath the entire facade was a totally different person. I had become a real hypocrite, an actor. I was careful not to reveal my true nature. I was living a lie. Underneath it all, I was a very unhappy, unfulfilled and hurting individual who was only concerned with his own agenda.

As long as I got what I wanted all was well. It is no wonder that our marriage finally ended. We separated in 1997 after twenty years of marriage. The main reason we separated was because even after twenty years of marriage, I was still thoroughly selfish in my sexuality and by this time I had immersed myself in transgendered desires. I had become totally bound to my wicked and selfish motivations. My mind was consistently given over only to the desires of the flesh. I could think of nothing else. I now not only wanted to dress as a woman, I wanted to become a woman.

Every waking moment became devoted to that end. I had turned from the Lord that I had always confessed as my Saviour, which I believe was due to the lack of Bible reading and personal Bible study, (also a lack of prayer) and now my sinful desire had brought me to the place that I went into even deeper darkness and joined a transgender club called Illusions.

Illusions was a club for men who were transvestites or trans-sexuals who could live out their perversions in the privacy and secrecy of a closed club. I attended this club against the will of my wife, ignoring her needs and the needs of my children. During the years I spent in this club I received a popularity that I never had while living as male, even being crowned 'Empress VI of Illusions.' The spirit that drove me well knew how one with no self-esteem could be puffed up with himself. I had a sense that in all of my days on this earth I had not experienced any kind of true fulfilment in life. The transgendered spirit gave me a false sense of self-value and wellness that twisted my deceived heart and mind in its wicked tentacles making me a true child of Hell. And I didn't even realize the danger of my choices.

My life went from believing in Jesus as a child to believing only in myself as an adult. On July 7th 2003 I underwent gender reassignment surgery in Montreal, Quebec under the name of Leslie Diane Montgomery. My life was ruined. I didn't realize it at the time but I know now that I was lost. I lived totally as a woman for ten years – 1997 to 2007. As time passed I began to feel very guilty and convicted about everything I had done to my family, my God and myself. I knew in my heart all the time that what I had done was wrong but just like the Scriptures say I suppressed the truth.

In the summer of 2007 the Spirit of God began to move in my heart, and I turned to the book of Romans. I knew that my life was in a helpless state, and it was the book of Romans that always seemed to give me hope. As I read and studied the Scriptures I came to know that I could no longer continue the charade that had cost me everything that I truly loved in life – my family and mostly my God. I finally cried out to God for mercy and asked Him to save me from myself. With the help of my dear friends Richard and his wonderful wife Marie I went shopping for male clothes to begin my life over. Before the end of the year I cut my hair and began to live my life as the man that God had made me to be.

It hasn't been easy. I continued to deal with debilitating depression, which developed during those years. But one of the best things that has happened since was that I started reading my Bible most days for at least an hour. Through that practice God has done a new work in me, which was far more than any medication could do. It has lifted me high above my depression and truly given me a new life. Jesus the Good Shepherd truly left the ninety and nine and graciously brought me back into the love and safety of His fold. I that was lost was found, to the Glory of my God and Savior, the Lord Jesus Christ.

I give God all the glory and honour for lifting me out of the muck and the mire of the world and setting me on the path that leads to His eternal Kingdom of Heaven.[1]

## Romans and a Renewed Mind

That was quite a testimony, wasn't it? It reminds us just how wrong the lie is that we so often hear today that people cannot change. The truth is, they can change, and they can change to the uttermost.

Leslie's story is not just a fascinating journey. It is ultimately about the power of God's sovereign grace in the gospel of Jesus Christ. There has been much hurt from his decision to leave his wife and children. And there's much to lament in his testimony when he talks about the delusion of transgender identity, which led him to try to remove all physical evidences of his God-given manhood and replace it with a womanly body and lifestyle. Of course, Leslie was still a man. Surgery couldn't change that. It simply scarred his body

---

1   We requested this testimony, but did not shape or alter it in any way. It is a real story of deliverance from sin; Gavin has counseled Leslie for years now in his fight against the flesh.

and confused his mind further. We grieve here. But praise God for His mercy!

When he was at rock bottom, Leslie opened the book of Romans. There he was shown how he had sinned against God and sat under His condemnation and how God offers a way to be right with Him through Jesus. The Apostle Paul phrases it like this: 'For there is no distinction: for all have sinned and fall short of the glory of God, and are justified by His grace as a gift, through the redemption that is in Christ Jesus' (Rom. 3:23-24). His Romans experience caused Leslie to repent of his sin and believe upon Jesus and His redeeming work on the cross. He trusted that (1) in Jesus righteous life was credited to him and (2) in Jesus' wrath-absorbing death on his behalf, he could be forgiven, declared right before God and adopted as a child of the Father. Leslie was lost and then found. But it didn't stop there.

In the first eleven chapters of Romans, Paul lays out God's mercies in the gospel. Then beginning in Chapter 12, based on the work of God *for* us, he sets forth what the work of God *in* us looks like. And the gospel that saved Leslie began to transform him: all of him. Notice Paul's words, 'I appeal to you therefore, brothers, by the mercies of God, to present your bodies as a living sacrifice, holy and acceptable to God, which is your spiritual worship. Do not be conformed to this world, but be transformed by the renewal of your mind, that by testing you may discern what is the will of God, what is good and acceptable and perfect' (Rom. 12:1-2).

In our discussion on transgenderism it is strikingly relevant to see that Paul authoritatively tells believers to present the *body* as a 'living sacrifice.' This is not an option. The exhortation contains divine authority. The embodied self, as male or female, with its desires and behaviors, belongs to the Lord and is to be used according to His will. It is a crucial mistake to view the Christian life with a bifurcation of the material and spiritual. Transgenderism is a modern form of an old heresy – Gnosticism. Gnosticism says that the material world is evil and the non-material world is good, and that one's secret knowledge is the key to salvation. However, in line with gnostic thinking, transgenderism ideology says that our bodies are not telling us anything about our identity as either male or female in God's image. Our identity is found in knowledge beyond that – a secret, subjective sense from within.[2]

---

2    Andrew Walker makes this point in *God and the Trans-gender Debate: What Does the Bible Actually Say About Gender Identity?* (Epsom: Surrey, The Good Book Company, 2017), pp. 25-6.

But this is not the way of a Christian. The Christian presents his or her whole self to God – body, mind and soul. This Christian lifestyle is described as 'spiritual' (*logikos*) worship. In other words, it is intelligent and informed according to the knowledge of God, the gospel and all of Scripture. This is not speaking of Sunday morning worship only but every detail in all of life. What we do with our bodies matters to God. And we discern God's good will with a renewed mind. That's why the worship is '*logikos*' – true spiritual worship is rational or informed, shaped by a renewed mind, the mind of the Spirit. What a gift God has given us!

## Change the Body—Or Change the Mind?

Our culture commonly counsels those who experience gender dysphoria to change the body to suit the mind. But the Biblical answer is to change the mind to suit the body. Transgender surgery is not the answer to the inner sense that you are trapped in the body of the opposite sex. Transgender lifestyle is not the answer. Conforming to worldly thinking and acting is not the answer. Transformation of the mind is the answer – an inside-out renewal is needed. A renewed mind is then able to see and do God's will: this transformation involves desires and actions. And the action is ongoing. It is a 'renewing of the mind.'

The Christian must carry on reorienting the mind away from old thinking patterns and onto new, God-centered thinking patterns.

Transgenderism goes against what is natural in God's creation design, just as homosexuality does. This is what we read in Romans 1:26-27, 'For this reason God gave them up to dishonorable passions. For their women exchanged natural relations for those that are contrary to nature; and the men likewise gave up natural relations with women and were consumed with passion for one another, men committing shameless acts with men and receiving in themselves the due penalty for their error.' It's the same idea with transgenderism. There is an exchanging of what is natural for what is unnatural. Hence it is described as an 'abomination' in Deuteronomy 22:5. Doing what is against nature is part of a pagan lifestyle (see Chapter 1).[3] The gospel, however, renews our minds to what is 'spiritual'

---

3  Nor should we miss that such behavior is in some cases expressly spiritual in nature. June Singer argues as follows: '[t]he archetype of androgyny appears in us as an innate sense of ... and witness to ... the primordial Cosmic unity, that is, it is the sacrament of monism, functioning to erase distinction ... [this was] nearly totally expunged from the Judeo-Christian tradition ... and a patriarchal God-image.' June Singer, *Androgyny: Towards a New Theory of Sexuality* (London: Routledge and Kegan, 1977), pp. 20, 22.

worship (Rom. 12:1) and to the will of God (Rom. 12:2).

As we have previously set out, this certainly includes the natural *complementary unity, polarity, and reciprocity*[4] God ordains at creation – which means we joyfully embrace God's design as image-bearing men and women. Our minds direct what we do with our bodies. Our function flows out of where our mind finds our identity. The gospel uproots our identity from being in Adam and replants it in Christ (see Rom. 5:12-21). That is why at the beginning of Romans 6 Paul gives this exhortation:

> What shall we say then? Are we to continue in sin that grace may abound? By no means! How can we who died to sin still live in it? Do you not know that all of us who have been baptized into Christ Jesus were baptized into His death? We were buried therefore with Him by baptism into death, in order that, just as Christ was raised from the dead by the glory of the Father, we too might walk in newness of life. (Rom. 6:1-4).

This means that if you are a 'transgender woman' (a biological male presenting as female) who is saved

---

4   Owen Strachan and Gavin Peacock, *What Does the Bible Teach About Lust?*, Biblical Sexuality Trilogy (Fearn: Ross-shire, Christian Focus, 2020). See the discussion in the previous chapter.

from death in Adam to life in Christ, you must and can now live as the man God created you to be. You can now fight disordered desires if and when they appear. The same is true for a 'transgender man' (a biological female presenting as a male). She must and can live as she was created – a woman who can fight disordered desires if and when they appear. In this way the person who has lived a transgender lifestyle or even had gender reassignment surgery is the same as any other Christian. They have turned their back on the old life and they are living in their new identity, with a renewed mind that is still renewing, presenting their bodies to God and doing His will with their bodies.

For a person to be saved and follow a transgender lifestyle is a *non sequitur* according to Paul. The whole body is to be presented to God in obedience. God doesn't command His children to do something He will not equip them to do. Complementary unity, polarity, and reciprocity represent God's standard for every believer.[5] To

---

5    Some might think we are speaking here of 'restoration' to divine design. As a fine point, we are not simply 'restored' to creational norms; we are conformed to the pattern of the new creation man or the new creation woman, an antitype of which pre-fall Adam and Eve are the type.

that end did you notice what Leslie says in his testimony after God saved him? 'I went shopping for male clothes to begin my life over. Before the end of the year I cut my hair and began to live my life as the man that God had made me to be.' What an example of the power of the gospel that saved and transformed a man! Yet we sometimes hear from Christian theologians and counsellors that no such changes are necessary. Leslie, reading the Bible for himself, knew otherwise.

With this in mind, for the rest of the chapter we will look at some key passages that lay out principles of Christ-empowered, God-honouring biblical manhood and womanhood. As we do this, we simultaneously affirm that we will be at our most happy when we live in accordance with the truth and reality of our identity as image-bearing Christian men or women. There isn't a more purposeful identity than this.

## What Are Biblical Manhood and Womanhood?

I speak to many men's groups and I often begin with the question, 'What is it to be a man and not a woman?' The common answer comes back: 'To be kind, joyful, peaceful, loving…' and so on. 'But that is a description of a Christian man or woman in general' is my response. 'What is it to be a man and *not* a woman? Or vice versa? What's the difference? Can you explain it and can you teach it to your children?'

The inability to answer this question with biblical accuracy has fueled many problems in the church today. Because we often cannot explain the complementary differences in manhood or womanhood from nature in creation applying in some way to all of life—not just the home and church—we have not been able to give a robust reply to the LGBTQ ideology that presses into all of life.

We dealt with creation foundations in Chapter 1 from which I will offer two creation observations on manhood and womanhood in order to build some definitions. The first creation observation is that manliness and womanliness flows from being made a man or woman. To put it another way, how a man or woman thinks and acts proceeds from who they are, constituted by God as male not female or vice versa (Gen. 1:27). We read that God made man male and female and immediately after that He says, 'Be fruitful and multiply' (Gen. 1:28). The complementary male-female functions in sexual union flow directly from the created sex.

This leads to a second creation observation. Manliness and womanliness mean at heart male leadership and female helping. It is noteworthy that both the man and the woman are charged with the dominion-taking task in Genesis 1:28, but we must see that the man, Adam, is to lead. Eve is the helper to him not the other way around (Gen. 2:18).

We can summarize manhood like this: God constituted the man to act out his manliness. It is not something abstract but tangible and visible. Manliness is something objective. Therefore, godly manliness means exercising courageous, benevolent dominion in his designated spheres of influence in order to bear fruit for the good of others. Within those spheres, manliness involves spiritual and physical leadership exhibited as protection and provision for those in his care, particularly women and children and especially for a wife.

In complementary fashion we can summarize womanhood like this: God constituted the woman to act out her womanliness. It is not something abstract but tangible and visible. Womanliness is something objective. Therefore, godly femininity means joyful helping by exercising gracious dominion as a life-giver in her various spheres of influence. Within those spheres she gladly respects and encourages appropriate manly spiritual and physical protection and provision, especially in submission to her husband.

We now turn to several New Testament texts, which outline this kind of manhood and woman-hood in the complementary polarity and reciprocity of the sexes.

## A Display of Godly Strength: Biblical Manhood

### (i) Mature Courage

'Be watchful, stand firm in the faith, act like men, be strong. Let all that you do be done in love' (1 Cor. 16:13-14).

When I was small and my father used to go away for work overnight, he would say to me, 'You're the man of the house now. Look after your mother and younger sister.' I'll always remember that. It gave me a sense of what I should be – as he drove away my little chest puffed out and I felt like a knight protecting a kingdom. Of course, at six years old I had only a fraction of the physical strength and mental ability of my mother. Nevertheless, something inside me stirred. This is what I was called to do – act like a man and protect the women from harm.

Spiritual immaturity and men who were not playing the man had marked the church in Corinth. They had, in a cowardly way like Adam, retreated from their duties and were embracing the Corinthian lifestyle, which promoted a pagan interchangeability and fluidity of the sexes. Relevant to our discussion, Paul warns them that homosexuals (including the effeminate man as argued in Book Two of this trilogy) will not enter heaven and exhorts men not to wear long hair like a woman (1 Cor. 11:14). Then he gives a short portrait of courageous, mature manhood. This is what a Christian man is like to some degree. And this is what the gospel transforms men to be. Tom Schreiner puts it well as he writes on an earlier passage in 1 Corinthians 11: 'Paul argues from creation, not from the fall. The distinctions between male and female are part of the created order, and Paul apparently didn't think redemption in Christ negated creation.'[6] So in the power of the gospel Paul exhorts the men of Corinth to habitual—creational—manliness.

There are five imperatives in Paul's exhortation and the central one is 'act like men.' It means to *behave with manly courage and maturity*. Even as he calls all believers to maturity there is a way a man must be an example of courage in the church. To put it another way, there is a certain maturity that men

---

6    Thomas R. Schreiner, 'Head Coverings, Prophecies and the Trinity', *Recovering Biblical Manhood and Womanhood*, p. 133. This relates to what we mentioned a few pages ago: salvation is *more* than restoration of creation, but it is surely not *less* than restoration of creation.

should exhibit which expresses itself in frontline bravery.[7] Courage like this is essential to manhood.

That is not to say women must not be courageous. There are many biblical examples of women who show courage: Sarah, Abigail, Deborah, Ruth, Esther, and Mary all rate here. At times women needed to display manly courage when they were alone or when men failed to step in and lead. In the same way, a mother will be the one to protect her children from violent assault if her husband is absent. However, there is a frontline sacrificial courage that protects women (and children), which is essential to mature manhood in a way it is not to womanhood. That's why, as he galvanizes the men for spiritual warfare, Paul says, 'Act like men,' and doesn't say, 'Act like women.' Effeminacy in a man is wrong in every form. To be sure the apostle says in other places that he was like a nursing mother, indicating his selfless care towards the church (1 Thess. 2:7). But he was not a mother. He was a father (1 Cor. 4:15). He was masculine and not feminine. To act the woman is not what is in view here. To play the man is.

---

7  Strachan, *Reenchanting Humanity* (Fearn: Christian Focus, 2019), p. 165. The fact that the root of this word is grounded in maleness suggests that men are expected to be the model of courage in the Christian community. As covered above.

The phrase 'act like men' (ἀνδρίζομαι) occurs in the New Testament only here. Its etymology is from the root ανδρ. This is where we get ἀνήρ, 'man'. So 'act like men' is used predominantly of males. Solomon is told by his dying father, King David, 'I am about to go the way of all the earth. Be strong, and show yourself a man …' (1 Kings 2:2). David's instruction to Solomon is distinctly masculine, 'prove yourself a man' (1 Kings 2:2). That means there is particular behavior that befits a man that is different than that of a woman.

David unpacks this in the context of righteous leadership involving sacrificial mercy, providing and protecting for the sons of Barzillai, and exacting justice upon Joab and Shimei (1 Kings 2:5-9). He teaches Solomon what it means to be a man. Acting like a man means brave decision-making in order to exercise gracious lordship and dominion in his life. 'Act like men' also has the sense of being mature. Boys blame-shift. Men take responsibility and initiative. They act. And they act in a way that marks mature manhood – courageous leadership. Where Adam was fearfully passive, true masculinity shows humble courage.

For a man who experiences gender dysphoria, who cross-dresses or who has even had 'gender reassignment' surgery, the gospel is powerful good news. Not only are his sins forgiven in Christ, his mind and body are reoriented. So now he *can* act like a man. Not to *try* and be a man but because he *is* a man. He may still experience sinful impulses from the old man that he was. But he now has the power to slay them and the motivation to walk in holiness and take responsibility to be the new man he is. He may bear the consequence of irreversible physical scars, which prevent sexual union with a woman or even the desire for it. But he can still act like a man towards a woman. Paul exalts singleness as good and encourages those who are given singleness with the fact that God gifts it (1 Cor. 7:7). It may in fact be better for him to remain unmarried (1 Cor. 7:8) and show single-minded devotion to Christ. But still we must recognize that marriage is the norm and thus for many—though not all—biblical manhood involves a *complementary desire* for marriage.

## (ii) Being a Husband and Father

'Wives, submit to your husbands as to the Lord, because the husband is the head of the wife as Christ is the head of the church. He is the Savior of the body. Now as the church submits to Christ, so also wives are to submit to their husbands in everything. Husbands, love your wives, just as

Christ loved the church and gave Himself for her to make her holy, cleansing her with the washing of water by the word. He did this to present the church to Himself in splendor, without spot or wrinkle or anything like that, but holy and blameless. In the same way, husbands are to love their wives as their own bodies. He who loves his wife loves himself' (Eph. 5:22-28 csb).

Before we make brief comment on this text we must note that there is something deeply meaningful about a man becoming a husband. What do I mean? When Jesus refers to marriage in Matthew 19, He cites Genesis 1:27, 'So God created man in his own image, in the image of God he created him; male and female he created them.' He then immediately quotes Genesis 2:24, 'Therefore a man shall leave his father and his mother and hold fast to his wife, and they shall become one flesh.' The 'therefore' in that text refers directly back to Adam's declaration that the woman was 'bone of his bone and flesh of his flesh' in the previous verse (Gen. 2:23). This means that the man and woman are related in the most profound way from creation—both in God's image—but her taken *from him* and *for him*. So that when a man and woman return to each other, as it were, in the 'one flesh' union of marriage it is 'a re-enactment and testimony to the very structure of humanity as God created it.'[8] When a man becomes a husband he is doing something that is intrinsic to his creation as a man.

Moreover, his manhood is tied to a picture of redemption because marriage is a picture of Christ and the Church (Eph. 5:33). In this picture we see a couple of markers of mature manhood that are worth noting. Firstly, mature manhood means a husband is the head of his wife. You'll notice that Paul compares the husband to Christ and the wife to the Church. So, just as the roles of Christ and the church cannot be reversed, so it is with the husband and wife. And the husband *is* the head. This is his position in the team, and he must play his role. Headship means leadership with authority. He has the authority, through his position, to lead his wife in a Godward direction. It is not absolute authority, but authority delegated by God. Thus, he has the duty of setting the spiritual tone in the home.

Secondly, mature manhood means a husband is called to love his wife. This involves giving himself up for her as Jesus did for His Bride, the Church. So, we see that his position as head involves costly sacrifice for his wife as he gives himself to the task. Nevertheless, the aim is her holiness, not coddling

---

8    See D. A. Carson, *Matthew 13-28*, *Expositor's Bible Commentary* (Zondervan, 1995), p. 412.

her or pandering to her sinful inclinations. In our passage Paul instructs a husband to wash his wife with the Word. This means he will take a lead in devotions. He gives overall direction for the family in decision-making. And he regularly takes the lead in bringing the Word to his wife in daily devotions and words of biblical instruction and, if needs be, correction.[9]

He is also to treat her as his own body, cherishing her by providing for her spiritually and physically. The aim in it all is her holiness and a clear portrayal of the gospel as she submits to his loving Christlike headship. This kind of man never leaves his wife or abandons his post because she is unlovable or disrespectful. Like Christ he perseveres because he is fully loved by God and can give unconditional persevering love to his wife. In this way, he moves his marriage forward in God's purposes.

Thirdly, manhood means being a father. All marriages should desire children as fruit (Gen. 1:28) and

---

9   These are not mere trappings of a husband's life. These are callings. Of course, as a humble man, the godly husband will also welcome his wife's wisdom, counsel, and gracious speaking into his life. As we make clear below, complementarian men do not want weak women as spouses; complementarian men seek a wife who is gracious, submissive, and utterly fearless in the face of Satan, strong in the Scriptures, not in the culture.

a gift from God (Ps. 127:3). We have great sympathy for marriages where it has been biologically impossible for a couple to have children for various reasons. The grief is real. Still there is great hope and good in adoption if it is feasible. With regards to children, both parents are the authority (Eph. 6:1). But it is clear from Ephesians 6:4 that the Father is the overall authority in the home and should take a lead in the patient and wise discipline and instruction of his children – 'Fathers, do not provoke your children to anger, but bring them up in the discipline and instruction of the Lord' (Eph. 6:4).

## (iii) Aspiring to Eldership

'The saying is trustworthy: If anyone aspires to the office of overseer, he desires a noble task.' (1 Tim. 3:1)

'I do not permit a woman to teach or to exercise authority over a man; rather, she is to remain quiet. For Adam was formed first, then Eve and Adam was not deceived, but the woman was deceived and became a transgressor' (1 Tim. 2:12-14).

Before we move on to define biblical woman-hood, we must for a moment mention the call to male leadership in the local church. In the same way God constitutes masculine leadership in the home He does so in the household of God. You see the parallel. The bigger family needs male headship too. The biblical qualifications are found in 1 Timothy 3 and Titus 1. I don't think there is a job or vocation or career where being an unloving, undisciplined husband and father in the home would exempt or disqualify you.... except the office of pastor. Paul makes the connection between leadership in the home as a qualifier for leadership in the church in 1 Timothy 3:4: An elder 'must *manage his own household well,* with all dignity *keeping his children submissive,* for if someone does not know how to *manage his own household,* how will he care for God's church?'

In 1 Timothy 3:14-15 he refers to the church as the 'household of God' and expands on the idea of the church as family in 1 Timothy 5:1-2. In 1 Timothy 2:12-13, he explains that only men can fulfill the office and function of an elder. Only biblically qualified men can be elders/pastors. And not only the *office* of elder is prohibited for women it is also the *function* of elder. To put this as clearly as we can: women must not teach the mixed gathering of believers. Paul gives a clear reason for this: 'For Adam was formed first then Eve and Adam was not deceived, but the woman was deceived and became a transgressor' (1 Tim. 2:12-13). The reason for male headship is rooted in creation constitution and order but also the fact that when that order is usurped it brings great danger and harm. The serpent ignored the created order and approached Eve not Adam in the Garden. Adam was head of the home, but the serpent craftily undermined that. Eve was tempted and did not ask God or her husband before taking the fruit. She then led her husband into sin. In other words, at the fall of man the good created order of God-man-woman-animal was subverted to animal-woman-man-God.

Therefore, the principle of male headship runs from nuclear household to household of God. If a man cannot manage his own household well and demonstrate biblical leadership then he does not qualify to lead the church household (1 Tim. 3:4). More than that, pastors are called to be *examples* of biblical husbands and fathers to qualify. Men must be *excelling* in the home in order to be a church leader. So, one of the great needs of the day is to equip men to do these things and even to aspire to some kind of leadership in the church, even if it is not eldership (2 Tim. 2:2).

What a noble picture of manhood God paints in the Scriptures! And the clarion call of the gospel to the Christian man is, 'Don't try to be something you are not. Be who you are.' This is very much the call to the man experiencing transgender desires or living that lifestyle. And this is our plea in this book. Come in repentance to Christ for forgiveness of your sins and transforming new life. And when He saves you, He will enable you by a renewal of the mind to overcome sinful inclinations and use your body for God as He designed. Despite all past sin, what hope there is for that man. Remember these words of Paul: 'Therefore, if anyone is in Christ, he is a new creation. The old has passed away; behold, the new has come' (2 Cor. 5:17).

Let us now turn our attention to the beauty of biblical womanhood.

## A Display of Distinctive Beauty: Biblical Womanhood

### (i) Being a Life-Giving Helper

'Nevertheless, in the Lord woman is not independent of man nor man of woman; for as woman was made from man, so man is now born of woman. And all things are from God' (1 Cor. 11:11-12).

When my wife gave birth to our children, Jake and Ava, I was present each time. It was a wonderful experience – though I'm certainly glad she was the one giving birth! It was amazing to see her grow those children inside her and then bring them into the world. Moreover, I was never more aware of our differences as a man and woman than in those moments. Throughout each pregnancy as her belly would begin to swell, I would ask if it felt strange and she would answer that it felt like the most natural thing in the world. This is something for which I was not designed. She was.

Godly womanhood doesn't dismiss femininity, but reaffirms a woman's creation design. The woman was taken 'from the man for the man' – that is, she was made from Adam and brought to him as a helper fit for him. In supporting his leadership, she would help him spread God's dominion by having children and multiplying imagers of God across the earth. Her helping role comes directly from her created sex. Of course, though she was in a foundational way dependent upon the man for life, ever since her creation a man has depended upon a woman for life. Her helping function rooted in creation should issue forth in her interactions with men in a broader sense. Whether she is married or not, she should seek to support men wherever she can.

There are some gray areas regarding positions a woman may hold in the workplace to be sure. Nonetheless, the performance of biblical womanhood entails finding joy in helping men rather than battling them or knocking them down a peg. As we have argued above, godly women help godly men act like men; this is a godly undertaking, even if the world may find little value in it. The world finds surprisingly little value in the intangible work and calling a Christian woman (married or single) performs; people may undermine and even mock biblical womanhood for its supposed servility and lack of agency, its humble nature and self-sacrificial bent. But women who love Christ need not care a whit about such mockery. They may instead take great comfort in knowing that not one moment nor one attempt to bless others is missed by God. He is the rewarder of the godly, and He will honor every woman who honors Him through Christ-shaped femininity.

The world may sneer at distinctly Christian women, but God is smiling at them.

## (ii) Being a Wife and Mother

'Now as the church submits to Christ, so also wives should submit in everything to their husbands.' (Eph. 5:24)

As we saw earlier and in this text again, in a marriage the husband is compared to Christ and the wife to the church. It's vital to emphasize that a wife's submission to her husband is crucial to the picture of the gospel that they display. It is a central feature of biblical womanhood for that reason. As Elisabeth Elliot says in her wonderful book, *Let Me Be A Woman*, 'Submission is her strength.'[10] In an anti-authority, abuse-aware age our culture might construe submission as weak and dangerous. But Paul knew of such problems in the Greco-Roman world. Nonetheless he called wives to submit to their own husbands with churchlike responsiveness, which honors the man's Christlike headship. This never would include submission to abuse or mistreatment or sin; these things needfully noted, the wife is called to submit to her husband in all aspects of their lives together.

Her example of submission is the Lord Jesus Himself who did not grasp at equality but humbled Himself before the Father all the way to death on a cross. In fact, His humble submission is the ground for His high exaltation (Phil. 2:5-11). The inner attitude to this outward submission is called respect. 'However, let each one of you love his wife as himself, and let the wife see that she respects her husband' (Eph. 5:33). As he cherishes her, she is called to respect him as her husband and head.

Interestingly, this doesn't depend on his amazing leadership but on Christ's call to her as a wife and the position of her husband as her head. It depends on a picture of grace rather

10 Elisabeth Elliot, *Let Me Be A Woman*.

than personal ambitions. It doesn't even depend on whether he is a Christian or not. To be sure a Christian woman should marry a Christian man. That's clear from Scripture. But what if they are both unbelievers when married and the wife gets saved. Or how about if they marry as professing believers but he turns out not to be saved and she is. 1 Peter 3 speaks to either of these scenarios and says: 'Likewise, wives, be subject to your own husbands, so that even if some do not obey the word, they may be won without a word by the conduct of their wives when they see your respectful and pure conduct' (1 Pet. 3:1-2).

Strikingly it is her conduct not her conversation that will win him. He's heard the Word already, but it is her respect and purity that serves as an evangelistic adornment to the gospel. It's magnetic. We will look at this inner adornment shortly, but we mustn't miss that all this is possible because she is like the holy women of old 'who hoped in God' (1 Pet. 3:5). Her hope is that God rewards the obedient, not in the sense of earning salvation but in the sense of grace given for obedient service and that He will protect her and provide for her even if her husband isn't living up to his duty well. Rather than weakness, this is a wife's great strength.

The godly wife respects her husband's God-given position before she respects his personality or performance: 'the head of every man is Christ, the head of a wife is her husband, and the head of Christ is God' (1 Cor. 11:3). The godly wife submits in love for Christ and God's order. Here we would add that in our egalitarian age a wife who submits to her husband is a very powerful evangelistic adornment to the gospel for the watching world. Such a disposition, a worldview really, marks off a Christian woman from non-Christian womanhood in striking terms. There is beauty in submission; there is power, even properly *evangelistic* power, in godly womanhood.

As we've already mentioned, being a wife flowers into motherhood. Her body submits to and receives her husband in the love of a one-flesh union and the fruit is life. She uses her skill and wisdom to help her husband in his tasks for the week. She teaches her children with kindness (Prov. 31:26). She has an inward focus on her home (Prov. 31; Titus 2:5) and God's mission for their family. From her thought life to her speech to her outward dress and behavior a respectfully submissive wife embraces true femininity and honors God's design.[11]

## *(iii) Being a Titus 2 Woman*

'Older women likewise are to be reverent in behavior, not slanderers or slaves to much wine. They are to teach what is good, and so train the young women to love their husbands and children,[5] to be self-controlled, pure, working at home, kind, and submissive to their own husbands, that the word of God may not be reviled.' (Titus 2:3-5)

Women are called to mature womanhood in the same way that men are called to mature manhood. The mature Christian woman is described as 'reverent in behavior.' The word for 'reverent'

---

11  We sometimes hear today that biblical womanhood— which surely includes the call to submit to a husband, and a gentle and quiet spirit besides—will keep women from finding Christianity attractive. But note Rodney Stark's comments: 'Christianity was unusually appealing because within the Christian subculture women enjoyed far higher status than did women in the Greco-Roman world at large.' For example, 'The Christian woman enjoyed far greater marital security and equality than did her pagan neighbor.' Christians did not force their daughters into early marriages, while 'pagan women frequently were forced into prepubertal, consummated marriages.' Rodney Stark, *The Rise of Christianity: A Sociologist Reconsiders History* (Princeton: Princeton University Press, 1996), pp. 105, 95.

has the sense of carrying herself in a set-apart fashion – a holy woman[12]. Whilst the office of pastor/elder is not open to her, countless ministry opportunities are. Dr John Piper has helpfully laid some of them out in list form in the magisterial *Recovering Biblical Manhood and Womanhood*.[13]

This said, there is a great need for older women to disciple younger women. There is clearly scope for how this might work out differently from church to church. But we need to be careful that any women's ministry sits under the overall direction of the elders. It should feature teaching on the whole Bible but with a focus on self-control, sexual purity, and being a wife and mother as per Titus 2. And finally, it seems that the text suggests a more informal small group or one-to-one organic ministries in the life of the church. The best Titus 2 ministries have that goal as their end.

## *(iv) Having a Gentle and Quiet Spirit (1 Pet. 3)*

'…but let your adorning be the hidden person of the heart with the imperishable beauty of a

---

12  See John Stott's commentary, *The Message of 1 Timothy and Titus* (IVP, 1996), p. 188.

13  John Piper, *Recovering Biblical Manhood & Womanhood*.

gentle and quiet spirit, which in God's sight is very precious.' (1 Pet. 3:4)

Eve forgot her God-given position, but true femininity is humbly content with hers. That's beautiful. If being a helper is at the heart of femininity, a 'gentle and quiet spirit' is the flavor. This is the phrase Peter uses to describe what God values most in women. The worth of the gentle and quiet spirit is imperishable. It's priceless. This is not just for wives; it should be cultivated in all Christian women. The word for quiet is used in 1 Timothy 2:11 and is prescriptive of humble, submissive women in the church.

We note at this point that a woman does not become a biblical woman upon marriage; instead, in ideal terms a girl receives training along these lines all her life, and grows into a woman of God as she matures. A ring on her finger does not magically make her a godly woman; following Christ by grace as a woman does. It is true that much biblical teaching on womanhood has connection to marriage and the family, yes. Nonetheless women who trust Christ, perhaps later in life in some cases, are women of God. They need training in biblical womanhood to be sure, but they are called, as of the moment of their conversion, to live a distinctly Christian and womanly existence.

They are indeed distinct from lost women. Think about what the Bible says about the foolish woman, the opposite of the godly woman: 'She is loud and defiant; her feet never stay at home' (Prov. 7:11). It's not simply that she speaks with too much volume but that she is restless, even boisterous. Her feet will not stay at home. She is out and about, not focused on her household and not content with her position. Her heart is like a storm full of uncontrolled energy. She won't stay at home because it represents God's main domain for her (not that a woman cannot work outside the home in different circumstances and seasons). She is unsubmissive to his will and will not submit to a husband. She is not pure in conduct but is on the lookout for other men.

Just as many men have no idea of what masculinity looks like many women have departed from the biblical flavour of femininity: a gentle and quiet spirit grounded in the fear of God, not the fear of man. At the fall, Eve was not content in her heart and instead left her position and elevated herself. She lacked a gentle and quiet spirit and didn't act like the woman she was made to be. Simultaneously, Adam lacked the mature courage that should have marked his manhood and propelled him into action to protect and provide for Eve in the midst of her temptation and error. He didn't act like a man.

The beauty of the gospel is this: 'For Christ also suffered once for sins, the righteous for the unrighteous, that he might bring us to God, being put to death in the flesh but made alive in the spirit' (1 Pet. 3:18). Where women who have been deceived and have refused God's design for them as women and pursued what is contrary to nature in a manly transgender lifestyle, Christ has stood in and taken the blame for those sins – and all in order to bring that person to God. Once in a right relationship with God, a woman with a renewed mind thinks God's thoughts after Him – especially His thoughts for her as female. What security for a woman, knowing that God's thoughts are for her good. That's enough to quiet the storm in her heart.

> How precious to me are your thoughts, O God!
>     How vast is the sum of them!
> If I would count them, they are more than the sand.
> I awake, and I am still with you (Ps. 139:17-18).

## Manly and Womanly Membership in the Church (1 Tim. 5:1-2)

'Do not rebuke an older man but encourage him as you would a father, younger men as brothers, older women as mothers, younger women as sisters, in all purity' (1 Tim. 5:1-2).

As we close this chapter we remember Leslie's story. Leslie, like all Christians, has found hope in Christ and he has found power for transformation so that he lives as the man he was made to be. There has been fall-out from sin. But he has found a home and a family in the local church where he can be a manly man once more. I like to remind him that he is a father in our church. He has much experience of life and God's gracious saving power – knowledge of which he has passed on to many younger than him in our men's group. He has warned us all of the delusion of sinful sexual desire and the devastation it caused him physically, relationally and spiritually. But more than that he has gloried in God's love for him in Christ and the great hope of heaven he has as he battles on in the Christian way. He is a trophy of grace in the local church.

Transgenderism is a false identity and tells a lie about God. But the church offers a home for all those who find their true identity in Christ and follow His good design for sexuality. The church is a family – the bigger eternal family if you like. But it is still spoken of in terms of gender relationships. The gospel doesn't obliterate sex (or the natural family), it redeems it and reorders it. You have mothers and fathers and brothers and sisters in the church. Therefore, married or single, a Christian man or woman can express their God-given manhood or womanhood as laid out in this chapter in ways appropriate to these relationships. We shall examine this further in the next chapter.

You are the sex you were born even if your mind says something else, or an ideology asserts it. So, come to Jesus in repentance and faith. He never turns anyone away. We recognize the very real struggle with this issue. Nevertheless, Jesus says, 'Come to me, all who labor and are heavy laden, and I will give you rest. Take my yoke upon you, and learn from me, for I am gentle and lowly in heart, and you will find rest for your souls' (Matt. 11:28-29). There is much grace in Jesus but there is a yoke. We do things His way and that is always for our good and His glory. Hence, He reminds us, 'Have you not read that he who created them from the beginning made them male and female' (Matt. 19:4).

This transforming gospel of grace returns us to beautiful biblical manhood and womanhood. You are male or female made by God for God to image Himself particularly in your maleness and femaleness. And God says this is 'very good' (Gen. 1:31).

# 3. NEW IDENTITY, NEW LIFE

In Chapter 1 we looked at the foundations of what the Bible says about transgender identity. In Chapter 2, through Leslie's compelling testimony and some biblical exposition, we saw the power of God in saving him and returning him to biblical manhood. You, the reader, may be someone like Leslie. We praise the Lord for His grace to all Christians. But here's the thing, you might still be experiencing gender dysphoria – those old thoughts and desires seem to rear their heads now and then (or more regularly than that). You hate that this happens. You don't want this experience any more. You want to follow Jesus and you understand that He calls you to live as the sex you are born. How do you move forward? In this final chapter we will set forth some helpful key principles to this end.

## First, Transgender is not your Identity. Christ is your Identity and Christ Guards your Sexuality.

'Paul, an apostle of Christ Jesus by the will of God, and Timothy our brother, to the saints and faithful brothers in Christ at Colossae: Grace to you and peace from God our Father' (Col. 1:1-2).

The Apostle Paul begins the letter to the Colossians with a statement about their identity. You are 'In Christ,' he says, in the second verse of chapter one. This is the way the Christian believer is most referred to in the New Testament – 'In Christ.' The phrase 'in,' 'with Christ' or 'in Him' or 'in Jesus' is used almost 250 times between the Apostles Paul and John. In his letter to the Corinthians Paul says that believers are new creations 'in Christ' (2 Cor. 5:17). As a pastor so much of what I do is reminding church members of who they really are and what this really means. This also means that there is no such thing as a 'Trans Christian.' In the same way, we must not affirm the term 'Gay Christian'. You cannot define yourself by something that is clearly sinful and for which Jesus died. You are Christian, or 'In Christ'![1]

---

1    One helpful resource on this doctrine is J. Todd Billings, *Union with Christ: Reframing Theology and Ministry for the Church* (Grand Rapids: Baker Academic, 2011).

**108**

There are so many benefits of being 'in Christ.'[2] It makes for a useful exercise to take each reference in the New Testament and see exactly what it means. It will change your understanding of your union with Christ from just being a theological doctrine to a dynamic relational reality. If you are a Christian, you are joined to Jesus Christ in an unbreakable union. But it is not a union of equals. You are united to the Son of God. I know this is a heady thought, but it is the (truly incredible!) result of the gospel. The dual graces of justification and sanctification plus all the promises of God flow from our union with Christ. This truth eclipses everything to which you united yourself before you were saved.

You are still you, but you must remember you are a new you. You are not what you were. Jesus Christ now defines you, not your sin or your achievements, your relationships, your social status or your ethnicity. He has forgiven your sin on the cross. Now your boast is not your achievements, but Christ. Now you are a child of God, the Father, you have an elder brother in Christ, the Son and you have a new family in the

---

2   We unpacked some of these benefits in Book One and Chapter 4 of this series, *What Does the Bible Teach About Lust?*

church.[3] This is a family where you can be a king or a commoner, but you are of equal value before the Lord to everyone else. This is also a family where everyone's citizenship is in heaven. All this, and more, means your identity must ultimately be in Christ not your sexuality. Christ is the center of your universe, not sexuality (including any remaining sinful sexual impulses and desires). However, although Christ is our primary identity our sexuality is very important.

In the first chapter of *Sex and the Supremacy of Christ*, John Piper lays out two points that undergird his essays and all the others within the book. He writes the following:

> I have two simple and weighty points to make. I think everything in this book will be the explanation and application of these two points. The first is that *sexuality is designed by God as a way to know God in Christ more fully*. And the second is that *knowing God in Christ more fully is designed as a way of guarding and guiding our sexuality*...Now to state the two points again, this time negatively, in the first place *all misuses of our sexuality distort the true knowledge of Christ*. And, in the second place,

---

3   This new family, of course, does not collapse or undermine the natural family. Leadership in the local church is based upon a man having a healthy marriage and raising his children well (1 Tim. 3:1-7).

*all misuses of our sexuality derive from not having
the true knowledge of Christ. Or to put it one more
way: all sexual corruption serves to conceal the
true knowledge of Christ,* but *the true knowledge
of Christ serves to prevent sexual corruption.'*[4]

I think this is exactly right and very helpful.
As image bearers, our male or female sex and
sexuality is designed by God to say something
about Him so that we might relate to Him. In doing
this He enables us to have imagery and language
through the covenant of marriage between a man
and woman to explain what is happening when
the Bridegroom comes to die for His Bride and
secure her good forever. Misuse of our maleness
and femaleness distorts true knowledge of God
and His saving grace in Christ. But being in union
with Christ means being oriented to Christ and
knowing Him, not just intellectually but also
affectionately. We increasingly love what He loves
and do what He commands and embrace how
He defines us. So, finding our identity in Christ
actually guards our sexuality in all purity.

Christ is fully sufficient and in Him we lack
nothing. This includes the ability to live life
as the sex we were wonderfully made. When

---

4   John Piper, *Sex and the Supremacy of Christ* (Wheaton:
    Illinois, Crossway, 2005), p. 26.

Christ, not your sexuality, is your primary focus then your sexuality finds its rightful place in the complementary unity, polarity, and reciprocity of God's creation design as opposed to pagan distortions (see Owen's work on the pagan roots of transgenderism in Chapter 1). However, this is the same for every sinner who comes to Christ in repentance and faith. Therefore, if you have been transgender you are not a special category before you are saved or after you are saved. Everyone is sexually broken and sinful. Everyone begins with their identity outside of Christ and holds a pagan worldview. Here remember the words of the Dutch theologian Abraham Kuyper: 'The fundamental contrast has always been, still is, and will be until the end: Christianity and Paganism.'[5] There are only two worldviews: the Christian (biblical) worldview and pagan worldview. So, there are only two forces dividing the culture and the church over sexual morality: biblical sexuality and pagan sexuality.

The truth is everyone needs the deep compassion of Christ, which drove Him to willingly die for sexual sinners like us. And everyone needs to be brought to new life and joined to the risen

---

5    Abraham Kuyper, *Lectures on Calvinism* (Grand Rapids: Eerdmans, 1931), p. 199.

Christ by faith. A transgender person who gets saved must then work like every other Christian to daily apprehend the reality of their identity in Christ and embrace biblical sexuality. So, Jesus bids us focus on Him and follow Him … united to Him.

But Jesus never promises an easy way.

## Second, Remember: Serving Christ United is not Easy.

'He has delivered us from the domain of darkness and transferred us to the kingdom of his beloved Son, in whom we have redemption, the forgiveness of sins' (Col. 1:13-14).

It has been said that, 'Idealism is a killer.' We can certainly apply this to the Christian life. Many Christians struggle because they have wrong expectations of being a Christian. They have an *ideal* view of how things should be and they forget that sanctification is a process in a fallen world. They forget that the power of sin has been broken but the presence of sin remains. So, when they experience sinful desires or seem to be fighting a particular sin with regularity they become confused or disheartened. They expect easy Christianity – an ideal life with no struggle or need to work for change. But the Christian life is not easy, and change takes effort and time.

Let me give you an illustration of what we are talking about here. The city of Liverpool in England is very much known as the hometown of the iconic pop group, the Beatles. In addition, Liverpool Football Club is one of the biggest and most famous soccer clubs in the Premier League and in the world, with a rich and successful history in the game. For many years from the 1960s–1990s the club would only appoint managers (head coaches) from within their own ranks – 'from the boot room' they would say. That is to say when one manager left the club or retired, they would appoint his assistant coach in his place. Or in one or two cases a senior player became player-manager. All this was because they wanted to preserve the 'Liverpool Way.'

The 'Liverpool Way' was the very highest standards of achievement, style of play and moral ethos that the club embodied. This is why they won so consistently and were considered best in that period of time. If you came to Liverpool as a new player (i.e. you were purchased in the transfer market from another team) you had to learn the 'Liverpool Way.' You see, new players would come to the club with habits from their former club that needed to be unlearned. They wore the Liverpool shirt as soon as they arrived. They were a Liverpool player with all the benefits that entailed. But they needed to learn the 'Liverpool Way.'

Now think of the Christian. Here's the analogy: you have transferred teams from Satan City to Christ United! As the Apostle Paul expresses it, 'He has delivered us from the domain of darkness and *transferred* us to the kingdom of his beloved Son, in whom we have redemption, the forgiveness of sins' (Col. 1:13-14). Christ has made the transfer happen and He bought you at the cost of His blood. This is your redemption. Your sins have been forgiven. And you now wear the righteous shirt of Jesus Christ. Before Jesus ever came to earth Isaiah prophetically spoke of this when he said, 'I will greatly rejoice in the LORD; my soul shall exult in my God, for *he has clothed me with the garments of salvation; he has covered me with the robe of righteousness*, as a bridegroom decks himself like a priest with a beautiful headdress, and as a bride adorns herself with her jewels.' (Isa. 61:10). Paul explains it this way, 'For our sake he made him to be sin who knew no sin, so that in him we might become the righteousness of God' (2 Cor. 5:21). On the cross Jesus takes our sin and its consequences on Him and we take His righteousness and its benefits on us. To put it another way, we put on His clean shirt of righteousness and He puts on our dirty shirt of sin in exchange.

We need to pause for a moment now, because our football analogy will only go so far. There are some vital differences to acknowledge. With a football transfer the player has merited his transfer and price. With a Christian transfer the player cannot merit his transfer and is not rich enough to pay the fee for being a member of Christ United. With the Christian transfer Jesus merits it and pays the fee. As a member of Satan City the player's wages were death and hell. As a member of Christ United his wages are eternal life and heaven. With the football transfer the player's work rate and ability determine his success and success is not guaranteed. With the Christian transfer Christ's atoning work and sanctifying power through the Spirit guarantees final success – '... he (*the Holy Spirit*) is the guarantee of our inheritance until we acquire possession of it, to the praise of his glory' (Eph. 1:14). With the football transfer the player and the club get the glory. With the Christian transfer God in Christ alone gets the glory.

So immediately we trust in Jesus we are counted as right before God and in a right relationship with Him – we belong to Christ United as it were. We are now defined as such – 'in Christ.' But as members of Christ United we now need to learn the 'Christian Way' and unlearn our bad habits from when we played for Satan City. Furthermore, Jesus refers to the Christian Way as a narrow way (Matt. 7:13).

Which means that it is not easy and there will be pressures from the outside and inside to tempt us to conform to the world and step onto the easy way (Matt. 7:13).

## Keep the Goal in Mind (Pun Intended)

Jesus also says that the easy way ends in destruction but the hard way ends in life (Matt. 7:13-14). We need to keep the goal in mind. But Jesus' perspective here means we need to put to death and get rid of old desires and habits of mind, as in the football analogy. When they were learning the 'Liverpool Way' years ago, I'm sure those new Liverpool players did many things on and off the field without thinking because of ingrained reflexes and habits they brought with them from their old team. It's the same with the Christ United team member. He or she will experience thoughts, or reflexively do things that marked them when they were members of Satan City.

If you have identified as a member of the opposite sex to which you were born and you have been transferred to Christ United you might still have thoughts and desires that characterized the days you were a member of Satan City. Just because these thoughts or actions are a reality to some degree it does not necessarily mean you aren't a Christian. Remember we are in a sanctification process. It can take time. So take heart. Nevertheless, we cannot justify our sin. Instead we continually resolve to turn from it. We build the discipline of repentance into our training program.

In Book One of this trilogy, I use the story of how I practiced turning with a soccer ball for hours on end as an illustration of constantly practicing repentance. We have consistently written in this trilogy that we must repent of the sinful desire when it arises, not just when we act upon it in our minds or with our bodies. We recognize there is a distinction between *experiencing uninvited transgender desires* and *acting upon those desires* by cross-dressing or having gender reassignment surgery. But we must insist that the uninvited desire still calls for repentance because the desire is sinful. It is not merely fallen, or half-bad. It is sinful. The object of the desire always shows us whether the desire is sinful or not.

If this last point sounds a bit strong, think of anger, a less controversial matter today. If a man or woman finds murderous, vengeful anger rising up in them without just cause, they must recognize that they have a problem. More specifically, they are enslaved to anger. It is so uncontrollable in their heart that they are nearly powerless to stop it. While plotting a murder is distinct from a flash of hatred, an out-of-control temper is sinful. It demands repentance wherever it arises, whether quickly or extendedly. It is just so with lust, with homosexual desires, with transgender desires ('gender dysphoria'), and with too many other sins to count. If we have trouble with this point, we will do well to meditate on Matthew 5:21-30, for it speaks to this very set of issues, temptations common to humanity.

Practicing confession and bringing it to the Lord the moment a sinful transgender desire rises up and seeing Christ's forgiving love at Calvary as you turn back to your identity in Him will be difficult to do at first. It's much easier to let sinful desires go without dealing with them because we are not acting upon them. But treating sin like this is like pulling the head of the weed in your garden but leaving it rooted in the soil. It doesn't deal with it deeply enough – at root level. Repenting immediately at the occasion of transgender desire kills the root, not just the fruit, of sin.

As we have previously noted this is the same for any sinful impulse in any Christian. It's the secret of unlearning the Satan City Way and learning the spiritual mastery of the Christ United Way. This can be a slow process; or it might be fast. Whatever the case, you (and all of us) will be fighting sin in some form all your life. Things will only be 'ideal' when we die and meet Christ face to face (or when He returns). Only then we will be perfectly like Him (1 John 3:2). But we will certainly change in this life – there will be fruit and there will be victories before the final victory. The sign you are a member of Christ United is that by faith you are wearing the shirt of Christ's righteousness and using Christian means to learn the Christian Way of righteousness and so put bad habits to death.

So far in this chapter we have (i) established that Christ is our identity but Christ guards our sexuality (ii) the reality life as a Christian means that we need to learn the Christian Way and put away transgender thoughts or impulses. Now let's continue to look at how this further plays out.

## Press on and Don't Look Back: Live in Grace not Low-grade Guilt.

'Not that I have already obtained this or am already perfect, but I press on to make it my own, because Christ Jesus has made me His own. Brothers, I do not consider that I have made it my own. But one thing I do: forgetting what lies behind and straining forward to what lies ahead, I press on toward the goal for the prize of the upward call of God in Christ Jesus' (Phil. 3:12-14).

These words are very instructive. At this point you might say that the Christian way as outlined above is too hard or impossible. Well, God never calls us to do something He will not equip us to do. Becoming a Christian does not make us passive it makes us powerful. It does not leave us subject to our remaining sinfully deceptive and demoralizing desires, it makes us actively destroy them. Continuing with our sports analogies, Paul uses language that helps us imagine the Christian life as a race. He tells the Philippians twice, 'I press on.' This is energetic work in view. The Greek word used here contains the idea of 'pursuing' something (cf. 1 Tim. 6:11; 2 Tim. 2:22), and in some contexts it even means persecuting (Phil. 3:6). It's an onwards and forwards action—a sense of going after something. That something is, of course, heaven—the prize at the finish line of the Christian race.

But heaven is not gained with folded arms but by pressing on. I'm reminded as I write of a personal Christian hero, the great Scottish runner and missionary Eric Liddell. Liddell, an Olympic champion, had a running style that epitomized what Paul is getting at. At the most crucial parts of his races, when he needed to summon extra energy, he would tilt back his head and his arms would flail like a windmill. You can imagine the look of strain on his face that changed to joy at the finish line when he won. This is the zealous effort we need to apply to the Christian life.

But Paul adds another nuance. We press on 'forgetting what lies behind' and 'straining forward to what lies ahead.' If you are running a race and always looking over your shoulder you will not be looking at the finishing line and you will lose momentum. Paul is not saying that your memory and remembering things in your past is redundant. It can be a good spur on as you remember God's grace in the past or what you learned by your sins of the past. A glance over the shoulder in a race can be a good thing. Leslie's testimony in Chapter 2 is a prime example of the positive effect of looking back. But the point Paul makes is that we should not be focused on our past in a way that hinders us going forward. Avoiding this releases us for the strain of pressing on.

We recognize that there are various outside factors which some say influenced them in embracing transgenderism. Some have pointed to sexual abuse as a trigger moment, others to pornography, others to rejection and loneliness, others to a desire for attention and acceptance. One woman said that after she was raped she connected the experience so much with being a woman she thought if she morphed into the opposite sex it would provide escape and relief. This is heartbreaking to hear. Feelings of guilt and shame, some as a consequence of our own doing, and some by the evil doings of others, can come upon us unexpectedly and threaten to overwhelm us. If we keep focusing on our past or present spiritual failures, or if we are focusing on fleeting feelings of guilt and shame, we have lost sight of the prize of heaven. These things will negatively affect our progress as we can find ourselves living not in grace, but in low-grade guilt.

So Paul gives two grace-filled reasons for why he presses on and doesn't look back. What does he do? Firstly, he recognizes that he is not perfect. 'Not that I have already obtained or am already perfect; but I press on to make it my own.' If you were not to press on it would indicate that you thought you were perfect, or preferred your imperfections (even the imperfections of dwelling on past guilt and shame). It can also mean that you don't trust Christ's power enough to change you. Being a Christian means you should have what the old writers called 'holy dissatisfaction.' That's healthy. The more you know of Christ, the more you want to be like Him and you see areas where you are not – so you press on.

The second reason Paul gives for why he presses on is that Jesus has done the work of making him His own and has secured the finishing prize of heaven by His death and resurrection. 'Not that I have already obtained this or am already perfect; but I press on to make it my own, *because Christ has made me his own.*' He puts it another way in Philippians chapter two, 'Work out your own salvation with fear and trembling; for it is God who is at work in you' (Phil. 2:12-13 NASB). The work of pressing on is done depending on God's power. So, God's grace is the power that saves us and the power that motivates us in the Christian life. He has made you His own and He works in you. Therefore, press on.

Paul was pressing on. We can sometimes forget that this was a man who pressed on in persecuting the church and killing Christians before he was saved. You can only imagine some of the sinful impulses, guilt and shame he might have felt at times even after he was converted on the Damascus Road. So, don't dwell on your past transgender life or a recent experience of gender dysphoria. Don't dwell on the many factors that might have been influential in your transgenderism. Deal with it instead. It is not your identity or orientation anymore. It is not unusual that you have felt that old pang. But it is something you must repent of in light of being in Christ and all the blessings you have. Pray that God will stop the thoughts and desires as you look to Jesus and take every thought captive to Him (2 Cor. 10:5). And as you do this believe He will increasingly change you. This is not false hope this is biblical hope. So, press on and don't look back. And part of pressing on is pressing into the church.

## Third, Press into the Church, For You Have a Family Where You Can Live out Your Gender Role.

'See what great love the Father has lavished on us, that we should be called children of God! And that is what we are!' (1 John 3:1 NIV)

'Do not rebuke an older man but encourage him as you would a father, younger men as brothers, older women as mothers, younger women as sisters, in all purity.' (1 Tim. 5:1-2)

A vital result of the gospel is that we are brought into the family of God. When I say that, of course, we think of the church. However, first let's consider where the idea of family comes from – and this is God Himself. God is Father, Son and Holy Spirit. He speaks of Himself in masculine and familial terms, Father and Son. In addition to referring to the identity of believers predominantly as 'in Christ,' another great New Testament truth is that Jesus, the Son, reveals God as our Heavenly Father.[6]

Amidst a devastating attack on the family in our day, with broken homes and absent fathers and with a loss of identity at our most basic level of being created male or female in the image of God, the Fatherhood of God is the stabilizing reality for us. Because we are Christians, we are children of God. We have a Father in heaven who works everything in the universe together for the good of His children (Rom. 8:28). He owns this world and He is *our* Father who loves us infinitely more than the best human father. Therefore, our lives are sacred and secure until He calls us home to heaven. No matter what our earthly circumstances seem to be telling us we are actually the most privileged of people. So we can have an otherworldly peace and joy and thankfulness.

Pause now: do you view God as your gracious heavenly Father? Do you view yourself as a child of God? God is like the father in the parable of the Prodigal Son (Luke 15:11-32), who graciously gives his son his inheritance. And yet when the son has

---

6    On the importance of God as Father, see Douglas L. Huffman and Eric Johnson, *God Under Fire: Modern Scholarship Reinvents God* (Nashville: Thomas Nelson, 2002).

spent it all and is on skid row and when he comes to himself and returns home, his father runs out to meet him and smothers him with kisses. When he asks his father to make him a slave, his father tells his servant to get a robe and a ring and kill a calf to celebrate. His son is not a slave and he is home. Later in the parable the elder brother refuses to join the celebrations saying, 'Look how much I've done for you and you never gave me a party.' And the father answers, 'All that is mine is yours.' God is an abundantly generous Father, and one of the perennial problems for Christians is forgetting to see Him in this way. Like the prodigal or the elder brother, we too often think of Him as a hard task master who treats us like slaves instead of a gracious Father who loves us as sons.

Adam was meant to be a son of his Father and live forever but through his sin he became a child of wrath. So all the sons and daughters of Adam after him would be born with the nature of disobedient children. However, God is gracious even still, and there is the flicker of hope in Genesis 3:15 and the promise of one who will come as the seed of the woman and crush the head of the serpent. And He comes. The Father sends the Son, and Jesus Christ, the eternal Word becomes flesh and dwells amongst us as the only Son of the Father full of grace and truth as He reveals the Father's heart to gather His children in (John 1:14).

He does this by crushing Satan and sin at Calvary, so that 'to all who did receive him, who believed in his name, he gave the right to become children of God' (John 1:12). As He did with Adam at creation, God stoops once more and breathes life from above into us so that we are 'born, not of blood nor of the will of the flesh nor of the will of man, but of God' (John 1:13) – and we become new creations (2 Cor. 5:17). We are spiritually born again into a new family with a new Father and an Elder brother and with brothers and sisters in the church—all of us filled with the Holy Spirit—all of us sons and heirs.

Even more than that, when we become children of God we automatically become related to each other. The church is called 'the household of God' (1 Tim. 3:15). And we relate in the church family in gender specific ways. As cited above, Paul frames it like this in 1 Timothy 5:1-2:'Do not rebuke an older man but encourage him as you would a father, younger men as brothers, older women as mothers, younger women as sisters, in all purity.'

For a transgender man or woman who is born again into the family of God he or she can live as their created sex – a Christian man or woman who lives out *complementary unity, polarity,* and *reciprocity.*

For various reasons a person coming from a trans lifestyle may never desire or be able to marry. But remember marriage does not make you a man or woman. You can still be a single man or woman and live that out in gender-specific, familial relationships in the church. You can live this way in the culture at school or work for sure. But the church is the teaching and training ground for this, as we will see. Being single is okay in the church but secularistic individualism is not. We are family and we are referred to in the masculine and feminine – fathers, mothers, brothers and sisters as Paul tells us.

## The Goodness of Singleness

We affirm that marriage is the norm and we should aim for it, but singleness is still good in the household of God. With that in mind here's a short discourse on singleness.

*Firstly*, Paul preferred singleness but recognizes it as a gift not everyone is given. He recognizes marriage and singleness as good – 1 Cor 7:7 'I wish that all were as I myself am. But each has his own gift from God, one of one kind and one of another.'

*Secondly*, it avoids trouble – 1 Cor. 7:28, '... Yet those who marry will have worldly troubles, and I would spare you that.' There will be conflict in marriage. You've got two sinners living together in the closest possible relationship and proximity. Singleness spares you those particular troubles.

*Thirdly*, it gives the chance of single-minded devotion to the Lord – 1 Cor. 7:35 'I say this for your own benefit, not to lay any restraint upon you, but to promote good order and to secure your undivided devotion to the Lord.' So, a single status enables unique attention to God's purposes without the duties that marriage brings.

John Piper distinguishes others-centered single-ness from self-centered singleness:

> Today singleness is cherished by many because it brings maximum freedom for self-realization. You pull your own strings. No one cramps your style. But Paul cherished his singleness because it put him utterly at the disposal of the Lord Jesus ... The contemporary mood promotes singleness (but not chastity) because it frees from slavery. Paul promotes singleness (and chastity) because it frees for slavery – namely slavery to Christ.[7]

Now, let's think about how Paul gets to this position on singleness in 1 Corinthians 7 with a quick Biblical Theology. In Genesis 1 we have already seen the first command given to the

---

7   John Piper, 'Satan Uses Sexual Desire,' December 9, 1984 (sermon), accessible at HYPERLINK https://www.desiringgod.org/messages/satan-uses-sexual-desire. Last accessed January 2020.

man and woman was to be fruitful and multiply (producing babies) and subdue the earth. Then Genesis 2:24, shows that marriage is the context for sex. In Genesis 12, God makes a promise to Abraham. It's a covenant promise. In it He promises offspring (cf. Isaac and Jacob, Genesis 26, Genesis 28). But Deuteronomy 25:6 says your name is *'blotted out of Israel'* if you don't have a child. Your name was virtually cut off from the earth if you didn't have kids (cf. Gen. 48:16). Singleness was, basically, a curse. Singles would include eunuchs who would most often have their sexual capacity taken away from them; it would include widows; it would include those with diseases like leprosy who were unapproachable; it would include those who were divorced and were not looked upon favorably. If you were a young man or woman, you were married as a young teenager as soon as possible because the blessing of God was evident in marriage and children.

However, we read in Isaiah 53:10: 'Yet it was the will of the LORD to crush him; he has put him to grief; when his soul makes an offering for guilt, he shall see his offspring;' This is predicting Christ and the cross but notice what he says, *'He shall see his offspring.'* Jesus is a single man, but He has offspring. Who are His offspring? Those whose sin He bore. The gospel of Christ multiplies the people of God, *not by physical procreation, but by spiritual regeneration* – by the new birth. You are not part of the people of God because you are born into a certain people; you are part of the people of God because you are born again, and this would change everything. Now watch the change. Isaiah 54:1 says, *'Sing, O barren woman …'* Why is there a burst of singing in celebration? Answer: because 'Your Maker is your husband' (Isa. 54:5). And He gives new life through His Spirit. Then Isaiah 56:3-5 speaks about eunuchs. The Lord says, 'Let not the eunuch say I am *a dry tree*' and says that their name will *'not be cut off.'* Why is this? Again, it's because the Kingdom of God is not dependent on physical offspring.

So, when we arrive at the New Testament and Matthew 19:10-12, Jesus says it's good to be a eunuch for the Kingdom. It's honorable to be single in these terms. That's why in 1 Corinthians 7 Paul talks positively about singleness (1 Cor. 7). The Old Testament people of God were multiplying almost exclusively through marriage and children, but now, the picture in the New Testament is the people of God are born, not of natural birth, but through the Spirit of the living God (John 1:12-13).

Biblically, marriage is definitely the norm in the Old Testament and the New Testament. It's a good thing. We should be preparing our boys and girls to be husbands and wives, fathers and mothers. The natural family is not replaced by the church, nor does it dissolve into the local church. It stands as an institution unto itself even until the end of the age. But the gospel brings dignity to singleness in valuing single men and women equally with those who are married. John the Baptist, Luke, Titus, Apollos, Lydia, Phoebe, Paul, and Jesus were not married. So, it's clear: while marriage is good and the calling of many in the church, singleness unto God is also good. Singleness allows the godly man or woman to display supreme satisfaction in Christ. Christ completes you, in other words, not a spouse.

Singleness portrays the Christian's ultimate identity in Christ, and a superior family in the church. So, Genesis 2:18 is still true, *'It is not good for man to be alone.'* However, no man or no woman is intended to live an individualistic life or be alone in the church; they have a family of brothers and sisters, mothers and fathers. Only the church is the everlasting family – all children of God the Father. So, there is hope for the transgender man or woman who is saved and can never have children or doesn't feel inclined to marriage even though they live out their birth sex in obedience to God. They might get married or they might remain a single man or woman. Regardless, the church becomes a place to learn and live out biblical manhood and womanhood in gender-specific relationships.

How does this happen?

## Fourth, Learn Habits of Manhood and Womanhood in the School of the Local Church.

In his book *Thoughts for Young Men*, J. C. Ryle wrote the following:

> Habits are like stones rolling down hill – the further they roll, the faster and more ungovernable is their course. Habits, like trees, are strengthened by age. A boy may bend an oak when it is a sapling – a hundred men cannot root it up, when it is a full-grown tree. A child can wade over the Thames River at its fountain-head – the largest ship in the world can float in it when it gets near the sea. So it is with habits: the older the stronger – the longer they have held possession, the harder they will be to cast out.[8]

This is true of good and bad habits and what we want to do is develop habits to make us effective Christian men and women in the church. Pastors take the lead here and preach the whole counsel

8   J. C. Ryle, *Thoughts for Young Men* (Lansing, Michigan: Calvary Press, 2000), pp. 12-13.

of God, which will include a diet of teaching either aimed at men or women from the text or angled towards men or women in application. A recovery of teaching on the Fatherhood of God is vital here. Very few scholars have or are even writing on the subject of paterology.[9] God refers to Himself in masculine terms and Jesus came enfleshed as a man. He still exists as the resurrected God-man in heaven, will return in that resurrected body and will always have it. That is a very good reason to believe we will still be male or female in heaven.

Teaching on the Fatherhood of God is so important because it is from knowing God as Father that we understand how salvation works. He is Father in relation to the Son and it is He who initiates and sends the Son to ransom sinners – who in consequence reveals the Father to us (see John 4; Ephesians 1; Hebrews 1). It is also from knowing God as Father that we understand ourselves as sons and heirs, children of the living God and a family in the church. Unfortunately, in many of our churches, in losing clarity on the Fatherhood of God (and Son as husband in salvation), we have

---

9   Here I can think of Robert Candlish, *The Fatherhood of God* (Adam and Charles Black, 1865). More recently there has been Ryan Rippee, *That God May Be All in All* (Eugene, Oregon: Pickwick, 2018).

failed to affirm the husband and father's central role in the home as loving leader.

Gender-specific teaching in the organic life of the church family is also therefore very important. Nuclear families should be structured according to God's design and must be functioning in that way too: husbands leading and loving wives; wives submitting to and respecting husbands; both as a picture of the gospel in godly manhood and womanhood. Children should obey parents who instruct them in the ways of God, led by the father. In the church family Paul mandates gender-specific teaching with older men being examples of godliness and teaching younger men, and older women being examples of godliness and teaching younger women (Titus 2:2-7).

One place this can happen is in men's and women's groups. In those times there will be natural discussion in consequence of what is being taught in relation to single or married men or women, or how we relate in the church. But there should be teaching on what are biblical manhood and womanhood specifically. In their book *God's Design for Man and Woman*, Andreas and Margaret Köstenberger keenly promote gender-specific teaching in gender-specific studies in order to develop habits of manhood and womanhood.[10] And these studies should have the goal of life-on-life, same-sex mentoring (cf. 2 Tim. 2:2, Titus 2:2-7).

Manhood and womanhood are caught as well as taught. So, a church that embodies biblical masculinity and femininity will be instructing each other. So, groups and events are not the goal – family life together is the goal. This will look slightly different from church to church. But principles should be consistent. As we interact with each other and share meals together in homes, we observe how marriage and parenting works, how spiritual mothers and fathers look, how care for a member of the opposite sex as a brother or sister works itself out.

We are always relating as men or women with each other in the family of God. A man or woman who has turned from transgenderism and been saved can then learn how to be a Christian man or woman within a big family, where we are all growing from manly or womanly immaturity to maturity. Also, an unsaved transgender man or woman who enters our church buildings should encounter Christ through the preaching of the Word and through the love of His people. We

---

10 Andreas J. Köstenberger and Margaret E. Köstenberger, *God's Design for Man and Woman: A Biblical-Theological Survey* (Wheaton, Illinois: Crossway, 2014).

should treat all people as image-bearers worthy of honor and yet pre-eminently as sinners needing salvation.

## Conclusion: New Life in Jesus

This first thing everyone needs is not actually to sort out his or her sexuality, but to find new life in Jesus. Those made in the image of God need to be remade in the image of Christ (1 Cor. 15:49). But once saved, as we have pointed out, there will be change. Christ will strengthen the believer as a man or woman of God. This may take time and will involve hardship. But if they are a saved man or woman, He will supply the power.

You may be a Christian reading this book to understand transgenderism and how to think and act biblically with regards to it. You might be a man or woman like Leslie, who was transgender and has been saved. Or you may be a transgender person who isn't a Christian but has been given this book by a Christian friend. Whatever the case, know that for all people our eternal destiny hangs in the balance when we meet Jesus. Life is very short and then we have eternity with or without Christ. Therefore, see this book as a message of love for all kinds of people and all peoples everywhere. For love's sake we want to see men and women, boys and girls saved and living out God's design for them and obeying all He commands, knowing holiness means happiness. And we know love rejoices with the truth (1 Cor. 13:6).

# FREQUENTLY ASKED QUESTIONS

___

## *What Does the Bible Teach About Transgenderism?*

In this section of the book, we address questions people frequently raise surrounding the issue of transgenderism. Our aim here is not to give lengthy and exhaustive answers to these good queries, but is instead to build off of the content of this book and give short, readable, practical guidance on these subjects. We cite Scripture as our authority and guide, but in some answers below, we give biblically-shaped wisdom where there are gray areas.

### 1. Our five-year-old son dressed up in his sister's princess outfit. How should I handle this?

He is probably just experimenting as all children do. He may be doing it out of interest and amusement or for attention. If it continues, you should gently but clearly bring such behavior to a halt. Use the moment as an opportunity to teach and reinforce how God made him a boy (in God's image) and is pleased when boys dress to show they are boys. Encourage him by showing how daddy dresses different than mommy and how he is like daddy and not mommy in this regard. Redeem the moment even as you graciously guard against flouting God's design (out of ignorance).

## 2. My eight-year-old daughter says she is a boy, wants to dress and cut her hair like one and she wants to change her name. She is insistent. What is my response?

There could be and probably are many factors influencing her, not least the culture that has made transgender identity acceptable and desirable. *Firstly,* realize and assume your parental responsibility and authority before God. She is an eight year old in your care, not the school's or the culture's. We don't let our children drink and drive and have sex until a certain age. She cannot insist that her immature will prevails against yours. At all stages of being a minor she doesn't have the right to change her name. You should teach her that it is the name her parents gave her as God's guardians over her and that it would be disrespectful to God for her to change it.

*Secondly,* use the opportunity to teach about God's design of two fixed sexes, how her body is given by God to show her who she is, how it is a gift to be respected, and how her expression of that is tied to her biological sex at birth.

*Thirdly,* you should take her back to the gospel. Whether she is professing faith or not show her that we all have disordered feelings that don't align with God's will because of sin and the fallen world in which we live, but Jesus came to redeem us and empower us to think and feel rightly.

*Fourthly,* it's a matter of parental wisdom when you let your child begin to have a say in what she wears or how she appears (eight seems way too young). But you ought to be affirming her femaleness by the clothes you dress her in. Gender-neutral clothing is becoming more and more the norm. We are not saying that a girl can never wear jeans and must be able to sit on her hair, and we certainly do not wish to over-stereotype so that a girl who prefers climbing trees to playing with her Barbie dolls might think she is a boy. But she should generally appear and act in biblically appropriate ways that express her femininity and distinguish her from a boy.

### 3. My child is 'intersex.' What sex should I raise them?

*Firstly,* a better term for this condition is a 'disorder of sexual development' (DSD). We commend the work of Alan Branch on this matter.[1]

---

1   See J. Alan Branch, *Affirming God's Image: Addressing the Transgender Question with Science and Scripture*

*Secondly*, this is not an easy situation in the rare cases that exist and requires much wisdom. Be assured that the existence of DSD doesn't change the fact that there are binary complementary sexes only. There is no possibility of a third sex. Scripture defines what is true and normative not fallen creation.

*Thirdly*, the entrance of sin has created ambiguous cases like this. The gospel promises the reality of freedom of the penalty and power of sin and the guaranteed hope of total renewal of body and soul (already begun) in the New Heavens and New Earth. So parents should try and find the chromosomal state of their child. If there is a Y gene then it is most likely a boy. Resist surgery. Don't rush in. Pursue treatment that is in line with Christian ethics.[2]

## 4. I am a single Christian mom with a little boy. How do I raise him to be masculine?

Teach him God's good design in Genesis 1 and 2. Show him that he is different from girls and the same as boys around him at school and in the

---

(Bellingham, Washington: Lexham, 2019). Branch's work is sound throughout and worthy of reading and study on the subject of transgenderism.

2   Denny Burk's section on this condition in *What Is The Meaning of Sex?* (Wheaton, Illinois: Crossway), pp. 169-183, is pastorally helpful.

church. Read him stories of strong and exemplary biblical men. In the family of the church let other men gradually have some appropriate influence on him. A single mom can also show hospitality to families within the church family and expose him to fathers and mothers in a nuclear household. This should be reciprocated but sometimes our singleness can paralyze us (and sometimes give us a victim mindset) and make us think people should come to us instead of going to others.

## 5. Should we use the preferred name and gender specific pronouns of a transgender person?

With regards to the name this could depend on the relationship. If it is someone you are introduced to for the first time, it is the only name you have for him or her. If it is an obviously masculine or feminine name applied to the opposite sex it might seem very awkward so you might avoid using it as much as possible. If it's a relative whom you knew as Jane and she changes her name to John it may be a different case. We know that on occasion followers of God were given pagan names (see the books of Esther and Daniel, for example). This does not mean that we seek to use names reflecting a sinful choice, for we do not. It does mean that the matter can be complex, and difficult to handle (as it surely was for the biblical

WHAT DOES THE BIBLE TEACH ABOUT TRANSGENDERISM?

figures we mentioned, living as they did against their will in ungodly settings). In some sense, we are all increasingly in Babylon.

When it comes to gender specific pronouns, it is advisable not to compromise. To call a man 'she' or 'her' or a woman 'he' or 'him' is a lie. And although we must remember that all sin is sin, not all sins are the same in gravity. Transgenderism is an egregious sin before God and tramples on His glory, for He is the one who created us in His image male or female. Affirming the opposite of that truth with the pronouns you use for that person also participates in the lie and that person's delusion and spreads confusion among believers in the church. So for the sake of love for God, the transgender person, and the church, we should not use those pronouns.

We can use wisdom and avoid using pronouns as much as we can. We certainly want to explain our reasons in the kindest way to the person and affirm our care for them. Nevertheless, we urge the church not to respond to public peer pressure on this issue, but to hold the line of truth for the sake of being holy and being a clear witness. We recognize this will not be easy in many relationships, for instance with a child who demands this and threatens to end the relationship if that demand is not met. We encourage godly fathers and mothers to express their love for their child but strongly affirm their superior allegiance to Christ. If we fail to do so, by our compromise we are saying that our child is more important than their God and that is neither God-honoring nor a good witness to the child.

As a final comment, we have mentioned in our book *What Does The Bible Teach About Homosexuality?* that where freedom of speech and religion is being eroded and forced speech is being implemented in many organizations, a Christian employer or employee, student or teacher, might well need to take Christian legal advice. This issue is close to the toughest one many believers will face in the workplace, and we need to be ready to stand for truth, and ready to take what consequences this stand brings.

## 6. What should Christian parents do when someone of the opposite sex is allowed to compete on their child's sports team and shower in their locker rooms?

We assume that the child is still a minor but in his or her teens as this is typically when the situation might arise with respect to showering. You can make the case to the team coach or organizers that biology should trump identity and that no one should impose upon everyone else the fact that someone else is confused and has a subjective sense of being something they are not. In addition you could state the fact that this is a same-sex team and the well-being of the group is more important than the individual's subjective sense of self.

You might attempt to gain some support from other parents but if the team organizers insist on this policy we advise that you remove your child from the team and an immoral situation. We would also hope your child would desire to be off a team which allows for a member of the opposite sex changing and showering with them.

### 7. Parents at my child's school are encouraging their child to embrace an opposite-gender identity. How should I handle this?

Here we recall the biblical precept we've raised already: you should speak the truth in love (Eph. 4:15). This does not mean being really nice and only telling people that God loves them and has a wonderful plan for their life. It means seeking to engage these parents in a respectful and Christlike way, and in doing so, making clear to them that they may be thinking they are helping and loving their child, but they are in truth harming their child terribly, sinning against the Creator, and must cease any form of encouraging the child to embrace an opposite-gender appearance and identity. Ideally, this will lead to an opportunity to share Christ, the hope of every sinner.

## 8. How should churches direct a transgender person with regards to use of toilet?

We do not wish to make anyone unnecessarily uncomfortable in our churches but we also want to do what is moral and doesn't grieve our own church members. So we would have someone show this person to a private bathroom on the premises. Then the transgender person will be comfortable and others won't be uncomfortable.

## 9. Can a person who had gender reassignment surgery but has since been saved serve as a deacon or elder in the church?

Theoretically yes. If he has mastery over transgender desires and lifestyle and if he fulfills the qualifications of an elder (1 Tim. 3, Titus 1) it is possible. One concern, however, is his reputation with outsiders (1 Tim. 3:7). This may depend how public he was about his transition and what kind of transgender lifestyle he led in the past. That said, Saul was a murderer of Christians and after his conversion he became a prolific apostle. So, we have a generally positive take on this situation with one or two cautionary words.

**10. We are members in our church. My husband is an elder. He has confessed to me that he is experiencing regular transgendered desires and has started cross-dressing in private. How do we proceed?**

*Firstly*, he must confess this to the elders and step down from his position. He is pursuing a sinful path, which disqualifies him from the pastorate. He is now not above reproach, sober minded or self controlled and not able to teach or manage his own household – to name a few disqualifications (1 Tim. 3:7). He is also abdicating responsibility to be a husband and father.

*Secondly*, he should be warned to repent of his desires and actions and enter personal and marriage counseling. If he refuses, sadly he should be put out of the church (Matt. 18:15-20; 1 Cor. 5:1-13).

**11. You speak about us not having the right visceral responses to sexual immorality anymore. If the Bible calls it an abomination (Deut. 22:5), should we be repulsed by transgenderism?**

The short answer is yes we should abhor every sin but love the sinner. We need to see things as God sees them and have both His holy zeal and compassion. This means we should be kind to transgender persons while not being agreeable with their sin. Jude speaks of showing mercy 'with fear, hating even the garment stained by the flesh' (Jude 23). We think this speaks perfectly to this situation. We show mercy and go towards a transgender person in love. But we guard ourselves from softening our comprehension of the truth as we do so.

### 12. How do we differentiate between those who are 'gender dysphoric' and the more recent culture of those who advocate gender fluidity?

This question doesn't suggest that it's acceptable to act on 'gender dysphoria.' It does, however, make a crucial distinction between such folks who go through psychological travail because they despair in their gender situation and those who are completely without such despair or pain and hold a philosophical position that sex and gender don't matter at all. These are very different positions with very different responses needed. We could add a third category – the transgender activists who are pressing the agenda into school systems and workplaces such that our children are being indoctrinated and confused and our workplaces are becoming untenable.

In all three cases, we should love fellow sinners and call them to the truth, to the gospel. We need to also distinguish between these groups. Some have gender dysphoria and do not know how to handle it; some have it and are fine with it; some advocate that having it is a good state that society should restructure itself to approve. We comprehend that there is a phenomenon called 'rapid-onset gender dysphoria' in adolescents and young adults; this is when a youngster identifies as the opposite sex because of the feeling of acceptance they get or desire of attention they want. We encourage careful counseling on this matter driven by clear knowledge of the truth and, specifically, of the sinfulness even of desires that bubble up within us seemingly on their own. We need to remember on this count that sin is not only what we ourselves think is sin; sin is any want of conformity to, or transgression of, the will of God.[3]

This is in truth our counsel for all who experience what is called 'gender dysphoria'; though circumstances and backgrounds and dispositions toward this experience vary widely—necessitating counsel and compassionate care—nonetheless the fundamental truth identified from Scripture in this book stands. We all sin in many ways, including in seemingly 'unasked for' ways, but are never off

---

3   We are using the language of the Westminster Shorter Catechism here (Question 14): 'Sin is any want of conformity unto, or transgression of, the law of God.'

the hook before the Lord.[4] When we do not think and feel rightly, we have strayed from God's truth; we are not honoring God as we should. Texts like Deuteronomy 22:5 leave no room for us to see righteousness in any instance where, for example, a man wears a woman's cloak. The old covenant law gave no exception or exemption for psychological reasons, though individual Israelites no doubt had a variety of reasons for doing such actions.

So, we encourage pastors, elders, and leaders to speak the truth in love on these matters. All are in need of the transforming power of the gospel, power that flows from confession, repentance, and faith in Christ. When we not only feel our 'dysphoric' experience but celebrate and promote it, we must recognize that we are in still graver circumstances, and are not only sinning against God through our ungodly impulses, but are making our impulses our identity and our cause. There is no fancy solution for such people; we tremble for them as for all fellow

---

4   See Reformed theologian Louis Berkhof on this count: 'Sin does not consist only in overt acts, but also in sinful habits and in a sinful condition of the soul. ... The sinful acts and dispositions of man must be referred to and find their explanation in a corrupt nature. ... The state or condition of man is thoroughly sinful. ... In conclusion it may be said that sin may be defined as lack of conformity to the moral law of God, either in act, disposition, or state ...' Louis Berkhof, *Systematic Theology*, new combined ed. (Grand Rapids: Eerdmans, 1996), p. 233.

sinners by nature, and call them afresh to trust Christ and leave their ungodly ways behind.

### 13.  If I want to find a church that preaches and teaches the doctrine this book unfolds, how can I find one?

We hope and pray this happens as a result of this little book. God loves the local church, and calls us to join one in membership (see Matthew 18; 1 Corinthians 5; Hebrews 10:25). We would encourage you to find a church that clearly and happily affirms the following: the Chicago Statement on Biblical Inerrancy, the Danvers Statement on Biblical Manhood and Womanhood, and the Nashville Statement on Biblical Sexuality.

### 14.  If we tell the truth about transgender sin, won't unbelievers tune us out, causing us to lose our witness?

There is no tension between telling the truth and loving fellow sinners. It is loving, in fact, to tell the truth. Our proclamation of God's teaching, then, does not get in the way of Christian witness. Christian proclamation *is* Christian witness. We need to supplement our speech with the fruits of the Spirit, to be sure. We cannot think that we should only speak up and do no more. We are called to be 'light,' after all, to shimmer with life and love and the beauty of holiness (Matt. 5:17-20). But do not be mistaken: the natural man does not receive the things of God (1 Cor. 2:14). People may well disagree with, dislike, and even despise us for telling the truth about transgenderism. They could even go so far as to persecute us, as happened with Christ, as happened with His apostles, as has happened to countless Christians over the centuries.

Come what may, we must not lose sight of the fact that we are called to speak the truth in love. There is no new mission for Christians today; there is no new way for the church to proclaim God's Word. Pastors must lead out in this great calling; if our pulpits are mighty in the Scriptures, our people will be mighty in the Scriptures.[5] It is true that our own context may have its own sinful predilections, but we must not overdo 'contextual' witness. While always taking stock of where we are, we must remember that every place and every people has a truly desperate need for God, His gospel, and His Word. This is what the church gathered is in business to provide; this is what the church scattered strives to declare.

In the end, we will not be measured by results in themselves. We will be measured in divine

---

5  To better understand how every pastor is called to be a theologian, see Kevin J. Vanhoozer and Owen Strachan, *The Pastor as Public Theologian: Reclaiming a Lost Vision* (Grand Rapids: Baker Academic, 2015).

terms by faithfulness to the Word of God, not any earthly metric of popularity, fame, or success.

**15. You've given practical counsel in Chapter 2 of this book, but as a counselor or discipler in the church I want a fuller 'method' by which to walk people through gospel transformation and the everyday fight for faith. Any suggestions?**

This book is a partnership; the method below is one we have worked out together based on sound biblical doctrine, and that Gavin in particular has identified and applied in his pastoral work with numerous men and women. We call it the 'Delineation of Desire' approach.

1. **Discern** if the person is a Christian or not. This makes a huge difference. If they are Christian they need discipleship and counseling. If they are not they need evangelism and conversion. The first thing anyone needs is Christ. If they are saved they then, as a new creation, have the spiritual ability to go on being transformed by the renewal of their mind (Rom. 12:1-2).

2. **Draw** the person out. Gather information about their background and current life situation. This shows that when you speak the truth you love them as a person made in the image of God and don't regard them simply as a project (Eph. 4:25). It is also valuable in seeing what outside influences

there have been upon their sin, and if there are certain trigger situations where their sin manifests itself regularly.

3. **Detail** the significance of the gospel and what union with Christ means. If not a Christian, call them to faith in Christ. If they are a Christian, remind them that God could never love them less or more than He does in that moment, that their sins are forgiven and there is no legal guilt for them anymore. And that they have both the freedom and the power to overcome sin and put it to death. But also remind them that they *must* do this.

4. **Delineate** the design. As we have discussed, take people to the framework of biblical sexuality. Apply their situation to the good and wise design of God, and show them how faith in Christ affirms divine creation for all who are a new creation in Christ.

5. **Detect** the flesh. This flows from point two. Knowing the person and their story helps detect what might be underlying sins beneath the sin. (Sometimes sins cluster together, and sometimes they come on their own, even as all sin is idolatry.) In light of the previous point and a clear understanding of sin, identify what drives their specific sin patterns: is it desire to be worshipped, fear of man, envy, vengeance, power that underpins the sin they manifest?

6. **Destroy** the sin. Once the person has identified sins beneath sin they are in a position to kill sin at its root. Realizing their union with Christ they can name the sin(s) and turn from them. This repentance must happen at impulse level.

7. **Draw near** to Christ. Put on Christ – put on the new self (Col. 3). The Bible is specific about putting on Christ and becoming that which we are in Christ. Help the person see in which particular areas they need to grow: gratitude (key with sexual sin), humility, patience, joy and so on. Show them how being in Christ produces this in them.

8. **Direct** them to regulate their Christian life with regular times in the Word and prayer, leading them to pray specifically that God would help them take all desires and thoughts captive to Christ (2 Cor. 10:5). Also encourage wise inclusion of others to whom they might be accountable in their fight for purity.

9. **Determine** to walk with them in the fellowship of the church, knowing that sin is stubborn and change can take time. And above all pray. Spiritual change is supernatural change. True, the person must work – that is non-negotiable. But as Paul says it is God who works in a person providing the ultimate transformation (Phil. 2:12-13). Therefore, it is to God that we appeal and in His sovereign grace we rest.

## 16. Is the view in this book the same approach to transgenderism that all Christians advocate?

Sadly it is not. It has become more and more common to see transgender identity and behavior either as a matter of 'diversity,' such that it is merely an expression of self that is not wrong, or as a matter of 'disability.' If sin is a disability, it's equivalent to an illness that we can see is harmful but are not called to confess to God and repent over. (To read more about these problematic categories, see Owen's interaction with Mark Yarhouse's conception of transgender in the book *Scripture and the People of God.*)

Sin, including the compulsion to embrace cross-gender identity and behavior, is by no means a matter of neutral or positive 'diversity.' Nor is such thinking and action a 'disability,' though it may feel like a sickness we can't get rid of. If we make sin of any kind an illness that we are not morally responsible for, we end up psychologizing biblical morality. We change what is theological and moral to something therapeutic and neutral. We take away agency and responsibility from ourselves. Our sins become something we can't control and won't ultimately answer for in God's presence. This is a matter of grave urgency for the church.

We should expect this kind of shift in a culture that has swapped out divine holiness for therapeutic wellness (see the classic book *The Triumph of the Therapeutic* by Philip Rieff for context). People all around us have bought into such thinking, and think they are freed from the duty of killing sin as a result. But we who love Scripture cannot affirm such an exchange. Doing so threatens to compromise the entire theological structure of Christian morality. Ours is not a psychological faith at base; ours is a theological faith, one with profound moral duties before God. We must approach transgenderism in this way to do justice to Scripture, as this book has pervasively argued.

## ACKNOWLEDGEMENTS

We wish to thank Willie Mackenzie for his partnership in this book. The team at CFP was characteristically excellent in their work on the project; we thank them for all their labors, with a special word of gratitude to Rosanna Burton.

Erik Wolgemuth provided terrific literary representation in this endeavor.

We thank the leadership of Midwestern Baptist Theological Seminary (Kansas City, Missouri) and Calvary Grace Church (Calgary, Alberta) for their support, and for slotting us roles that allow us to serve the church through writing. Dr Jason Allen is an exemplary seminary President, and Clint Humfrey is an exemplary pastor-theologian.

Our wives, Bethany Strachan and Amanda Peacock, persevered in a jam-packed writing season and offered encouragement throughout the process. We each send love to our wife.

This book is dedicated to two pastors who showed us how to speak the truth in love, and who warned against unbelief while exalting the gospel of grace. We thank the Lord for these faithful men. Also, to Leslie Montgomery: thank you for your bold and beautiful testimony of God's grace which leaps out of the pages of this book.

Above all, we thank the living God, and pray that He may continually forgive us and find us faithful on the last day.

### About the Center for Biblical Sexuality

The Center for Biblical Sexuality (CBS) is a new initiative from Owen Strachan and Gavin Peacock. Primarily a website featuring resources on manhood, womanhood, biblical sexuality, the family, and more, the CBS offers biblical and theological clarity on the most pressing issues facing the global church in the areas of the body, personal identity, and sexuality. The mission statement of CBS: 'To strengthen the church and share Christ's love by answering pressing sexual questions with sound biblical doctrine.'

At the website, visitors will find long-form articles, multimedia content, links to helpful sites, and more. Please visit this new outlet at centerbiblicalsexuality.org.

**Also available by Owen Strachan
and Gavin Peacock...**

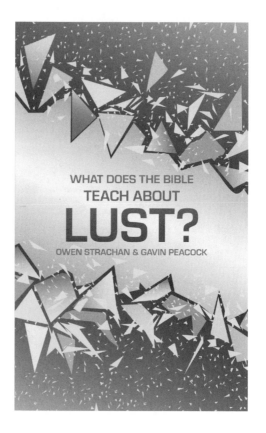

WHAT DOES THE BIBLE
TEACH ABOUT
# LUST?
OWEN STRACHAN & GAVIN PEACOCK

# What Does the Bible Teach About Lust?

## A Short Book on Desire

### Owen Strachan & Gavin Peacock

Lust is a problem. Our sexualised culture, promising freedom and pleasure, is creating a terrible cocktail of abuse, pain, despair, and suffering. The problem is not simply our actions, but our sinful desires. But there is hope. Christ is more powerful than any lustful desire, any temptation. He has defeated death and sin, and His way leads to true freedom.

978-1-5271-0476-1

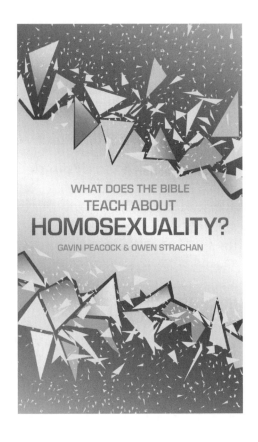

WHAT DOES THE BIBLE
TEACH ABOUT
# HOMOSEXUALITY?
GAVIN PEACOCK & OWEN STRACHAN

## What Does the Bible Teach About Homosexuality?

### A Short Book on Biblical Sexuality

### Owen Strachan & Gavin Peacock

God made sexuality. It is a gift and stewardship from God. But His purpose for our sexuality has been distorted by sin. Gavin Peacock and Owen Strachan encourage us to look at what God says about homosexuality, but also at the glorious truth of Christ's defeat of sin and redemption of our identities.

978-1-5271-0477-8

# THE
# GRAND
# DESIGN

Male and Female He Made Them

OWEN STRACHAN
& GAVIN PEACOCK